FLEXIBILITY IN EARLY VERB USE: EVIDENCE FROM A MULTIPLE-*N* DIARY STUDY

Letitia R. Naigles, Erika Hoff, and Donna Vear

WITH COMMENTARY BY
Michael Tomasello,
Silke Brandt,
Sandra R. Waxman,
and Jane B. Childers

W. Andrew Collins
Series Editor

MONOGRAPHS OF THE SOCIETY FOR RESEARCH IN CHILD DEVELOPMENT

Serial No. 293, Vol. 74, No. 2, 2009

Boston, Massachusetts   Oxford, United Kingdom

Andrew Fuligni
University of California, Los Angeles

Susan Graham
University of Calgary

Elena Grigorenko
Yale University

Megan Gunnar
University of Minnesota

Paul Harris
Harvard University

Susan Hespos
Vanderbilt University

Aletha Huston
University of Texas, Austin

Lene Jensen
Clark University

Ariel Kalil
University of Chicago

Melissa Koenig
University of Minnesota

Brett Laursen
Florida Atlantic University

Eva Lefkowitz
Pennsylvania State University

Katherine Magnuson
University of Wisconsin, Madison

Ann Masten
University of Minnesota

Kevin Miller
University of Michigan

Ginger Moore
Pennsylvania State University

David Moshman
University of Nebraska

Darcia Narvaez
University of Notre Dame

Katherine Nelson
City University of New York

Lisa Oakes
University of California, Davis

Thomas O'Connor
University of Rochester

Yukari Okamoto
University of California, Santa Barbara

Robert Pianta
University of Virginia

Mark Roosa
Arizona State University

Karl Rosengren
University of Illinois, Urbana-Champaign

Judith G. Smetana
University of Rochester

Kathy Stansbury
Morehouse College

Steve Thoma
University of Alabama

Michael Tomasello
Max Planck Institute

Deborah Vandell
University of California, Irvine

Richard Weinberg
University of Minnesota

Hirokazu Yoshikawa
New York University

Qing Zhou
Arizona State University

FLEXIBILITY IN EARLY VERB USE: EVIDENCE FROM A MULTIPLE-*N* DIARY STUDY

CONTENTS

COMMENTARY

Gift 9/09

ABSTRACT

Flexibility and productivity are hallmarks of human language use. Competent speakers have the capacity to use the words they know to serve a variety of communicative functions, to refer to new and varied exemplars of the categories to which words refer, and in new and varied combinations with other words. When and how children achieve this flexibility—and when they are truly productive language users—are central issues among accounts of language acquisition. The current study tests competing hypotheses of the achievement of flexibility and some kinds of productivity against data on children's first uses of their first-acquired verbs.

Eight mothers recorded their children's first 10 uses of 34 early-acquired verbs, if those verbs were produced within the window of the study. The children were between 16 and 20 months when the study began (depending on when the children started to produce verbs), were followed for between 3 and 12 months, and produced between 13 and 31 of the target verbs. These diary records provided the basis for a description of the pragmatic, semantic, and syntactic properties of early verb use.

The data revealed that within this early, initial period of verb use, children use their verbs both to command and describe, they use their verbs in reference to a variety of appropriate actions enacted by variety of actors and with a variety of affected objects, and they use their verbs in a variety of syntactic structures. All 8 children displayed semantic and grammatical flexibility before 24 months of age. These findings are more consistent with a model of the language-learning child as an avid generalizer than as a conservative language user. Children's early verb use suggests abilities and inclinations to abstract from experience that may indeed begin in infancy.

I. INTRODUCTION

Language knowledge in the adult is not a memorized list of words and sentences paired with the situations in which they have been experienced. Adult speakers use the words in their vocabularies flexibly—in novel settings and in reference to newly encountered instances of the categories that their words label. They can combine their words to form grammatical sentences that they have never heard. A central question in the study of language acquisition is when children achieve the context independence, extendability of meaning, and productivity of form that are the hallmarks of human linguistic competence.

One possibility is that children are avid generalizers who extend words to new referents and produce novel sentences very early in the course of language development. For example, a child who hears the verb *jump* in the imperative sentence *Don't jump on the bed* would without further linguistic experience also be able to use *jump* in declarative sentences, in reference to jumping done by other people, and even in reference to actions as different from the original as jumping up to reach something or jumping into the pool. Furthermore, the child would be able to use *jump* in other structures, such as *I jump*, *he jumped*, and *Granny jumped into the pool*. An alternative possibility is that children are initially conservative language learners who stay close to the examples of language use they have already experienced. A child who has heard *jump* only in *Don't jump on the bed* would not use jump to refer to a variety of other sorts of jumping, by a variety of different jumpers, or in a range of syntactic constructions. These two positions define a space that includes multiple possible descriptions of the child as language learner. In this monograph, we present new data on children's first uses of their first verbs and ask what theoretical positions within this hypothesis space are consistent with that evidence.

The view that children generalize beyond their experience in their very earliest productions yields the prediction that children's first uses of newly acquired verbs should be flexible, conveying a range of meanings and appearing in a variety of structures. The view that children are initially

1

conservative language learners yields the prediction that children's first uses of newly acquired verbs should be very repetitious in terms of the events they refer to and the structures they participate in because they are used only in contexts and/or structures similar to those in which they were first encountered.

Verbs are the focus of this investigation of the process of early language development for two reasons. First, verb acquisition has been less studied than noun acquisition. Thus, the rapid-generalizer and conservative-learner views of lexical development have been tested more frequently against data on the acquisition of nouns than verbs, and questions about the degree to which noun learning and verb learning are similar processes have been raised (e.g., Gentner & Boroditsky, 2002; Maguire, Hirsh-Pasek, & Golinkoff, 2006; Sandofer & Smith, 2000). Second, the development of verb use is also the development of grammar, by many accounts, because sentence structure is essentially defined in relation to the verb (Bloom, 1993). Thus, studying the acquisition of verbs provides a test of the rapid-generalizer and conservative-learner views with respect to grammatical development as well as lexical development.

Eight mothers kept detailed records of their children's first 10 uses of their first verbs over a period ranging from 3 to 13 months. Those first verb uses were coded for the pragmatic, semantic, and grammatical flexibility they evidenced, and competing accounts of the child as language learner were evaluated against those data. In the remainder of this introductory chapter, we present the theoretical and empirical background to this study in some detail, first considering work that addresses the extendability of verb meaning, second considering work that addresses the flexibility of verb grammar, and third, considering the theoretical and empirical background that yields predictions regarding relations among verb vocabulary growth, flexibility of verb meaning, and flexibility of verb grammar.

LEARNING VERB MEANING

Theories of Early Word Meanings

The child first encounters a new word used in a single utterance and a single situation, and he or she must somehow figure out both what the word refers to in that situation and what it can refer to in other situations. Current accounts of word learning differ in their descriptions of how the child makes that word-to-referent mapping and in how, and when, the child maps words not just to a single referent but to an entire category.

One view is that the child enters the word-learning task equipped with linguistic understandings that guide the mapping and extension processes.

Children understand, for example, that words refer, and this understanding guides them to seek a referent for newly encountered words (Golinkoff, Hirsh-Pasek, Mervis, Frawley, & Parillo, 1995; McShane, 1980). They also understand that words refer to kinds of things or events, which allows them to extend words to new instances of the same kind (Golinkoff et al., 1995; Naigles & Hoff, 2006; Poulin-duBois & Forbes, 2006). Children also bring syntactic competence to the word-learning, especially verb-learning, task. They use the correspondences between syntax and meaning to guide interpretation of the newly encountered verbs. For example, hearing a novel verb in a structure such as *X verbed Y*, yields, via syntactic bootstrapping, the interpretation that the verb is a causative verb (like *hit* or *kicked*) rather than a verb like *sing* or *laugh* (Gleitman, 1990; Naigles & Swensen, 2007).

Other theories attribute less initial linguistic sophistication to the language learning child and predict limited generalizations from experience in children's early word use. A child who does not understand that words refer may associate a new word with the entire context of its use (e.g., "open" applies only to what one's mother does to the refrigerator door; Dromi, 1982; Mervis, 1987). A child who understands only that words refer but not that they refer to kinds will construe meanings very narrowly. On some accounts, children, at some early point, tend to map words onto what is most salient in the concurrent context and to extend words to other things or events with similar perceptual properties (e.g., "open" may apply to lateral motions of doors but not of vertical motions of doors, lids, or containers; Hollich, Hirsh-Pasek, & Golinkoff, 2000; Maguire et al., 2006; Smith, 1999, 2000). All theories acknowledge that children eventually use reference, extendability, and syntactic information in their word learning, but some models hold that these biases and useable sources of information for word mapping and extension are not all available when word learning begins (Golinkoff et al., 1995; Hollich et al., 2000; Maguire et al., 2006). In this model, early verbs (those learned during the 2nd year of life) are likely to be used in specific contexts or extended limited ways based on perceptual similarity to the original exemplar. Only during the 3rd year of life can the child use social and linguistic sources of information for mapping and extension of verbs. Crucial to this Coalition-Emergentist model is the assertion that word-learning principles emerge earlier for nouns than for verbs and may not transfer directly from noun learning to verb learning (Golinkoff et al., 1995; Maguire et al., 2006).

These different models of word learning make different predictions about the degree to which children will extend their first verbs to new contexts of use and to new actions. A model that attributes to the verb-learning child sufficient syntactic knowledge to identify new verbs as verbs and sufficient lexical understanding to map new verbs onto categories of actions predicts that children will use their new verbs in utterances that serve a range of pragmatic functions and will extend the verbs they acquire to actions by a variety of actors or agents. A model that attributes less linguistic knowledge to the 1-year-old child predicts less extension of word use. The emergentist model (Golinkoff et al., 1995; Maguire et al., 2006) predicts initial conservative verb use followed by later flexible verb use. One way of testing these predictions is by looking at children's multiple uses of their first verbs. Do children first restrict the use of a new verb to a specific setting, or do they use the verb in a variety of settings?

Evidence From Studies of Word Learning

Questions about the extendability of newly acquired words have more frequently been addressed with data on nouns than verbs. Children between 12 and 18 months do sometimes underextend nouns, restricting their use to a single context (e.g., Dromi, 1987; Harris, Barrett, Jones, & Brookes, 1988). After 18 months, children's use of nouns in spontaneous speech is not context bound (Barrett, Harris, & Chasin, 1991), and in word-learning experiments children older than 18 months routinely extend novel nouns to more than one exemplar, even after only one presentation (Hirsh-Pasek, Golinkoff, Hennon, & Maguire, 2004; Markman, 1989).

If verb use also shows initial underextension, children might restrict newly acquired verbs to refer to a single addressee, actor, action type, or affected object. For example, a child might use the verb *blow* only when talking to Mom or only in reference to blowing out a candle, but not to refer to blowing one's nose. A child might know *sit* with reference to the dog's sitting but no one else's, or *eat* only in reference to eating pizza.

There is evidence of early verb meaning restricted by actor or affected object. Children's earliest uses of conventional verbs have been found to refer primarily to their own rather than another's actions (Childers & Tomasello, 2006; Huttenlocher, Smiley, & Charney, 1983; Smiley & Huttenlocher, 1995; but see Tomasello, 1992). Twenty-month-olds taught novel verbs via video were unsuccessful in understanding the extension of these verbs to similar actions performed by new actors (Maguire et al., 2006; Poulin-Dubois & Forbes, 2002). Diary studies have revealed other kinds of initial idiosyncratic verb use, such as *cut* used solely when using a knife, *watch* used solely when watching television, *push* used solely in a game of pushing in the pool, and *cry* used solely in reference to a pacifier (Braunwald, 1995; Smith & Sachs, 1990; Tomasello, 1992).

Evidence of extendable verb meanings during the 2nd year of life also exists. Children have been observed to use the same verb (*rock* and *ride*) to refer to the movements of both objects and people over the 6-month period from 13 to 19 months (Smiley & Huttenlocher, 1995). Laboratory assessments of children's understanding of familiar verbs have consistently found that toddlers demonstrate comprehension of a wide range of English verbs performed by unfamiliar actors (Golinkoff, Hirsh-Pasek, Cauley, & Gordon, 1987; Huttenlocher et al., 1983; Naigles, 1997; Naigles & Hoff, 2006), although other studies have found that extendability of verbs in comprehension is limited to children who had reached either a certain age or vocabulary level. Only children over 19 months and/or with high vocabulary counts extended familiar verbs to actions by unfamiliar actors (Forbes & Poulin-Dubois, 1997; Naigles & Hoff, 2006); further extensions of a verb to both new agents and new manners of action were found only at 26 months of age (Forbes & Poulin-Dubois, 1997). Exposure conditions also appear to matter. Twenty-one-month-olds who were taught two novel transitive verbs in a playroom setting with two different actors—themselves and the researchers—were able to distinguish those two verbs when presented on video with a disembodied hand as the only visible actor (Naigles, Bavin, & Smith, 2005), and the children in Naigles et al. (2005) may have been more accepting of yet another actor at test than children in other studies because the verbs had been taught with at least two actors.

Questions to Be Addressed Regarding Children's Acquisition of Verb Meanings

The previous literature suggests some early limits on the extendability of verb meanings and some increases in extendability as a function of age or level of language development achieved. There are suggestions in the data from Forbes and Poulin-Dubois (1997) that, in comprehension, extendability to new agents is an earlier achievement than extendability to new manners and outcomes. The existing literature leaves unanswered, however, several basic questions about the extendability of verbs as they enter children's lexicons:

1. How early in the process of learning verbs in general and/or how early in the course of learning individual verbs, does extendability emerge? The current study was designed to track children's extendability of verbs from the beginning of verb use in the child and from its first use for individual verbs to address this question.

2. Are some kinds of extendability earlier developmental achievements than others? If children use their verbs with different patients, affected objects, or different but still appropriate actions (e.g., *eating* cereal and *eating* a carrot; *opening* a door and *opening* a jar) it would indicate that the basis of their meanings is not closely tied to perceptual similarity (Golinkoff et al., 1995; Goodman, McDonough, & Brown, 1998; Maguire et al., 2006).

It is important to acknowledge, relative to both questions 1 and 2, that we will not be investigating when children can extend their verbs to *novel* actors, affected objects, contexts, and actions. Because we do not have access to all the verbs uses the children have experienced, we will be unable to specify the extent to which their demonstrated extendability goes beyond the input given. However, by noting when flexible use emerges in relation to their age and number of uses of a given verb, we will be able to address whether children's early verb use is more restricted than their later verb use.

3. What is the source of individual differences, among children and among verbs in the scope of verb extension? The comprehension data suggest age and vocabulary size as candidate factors with respect to individual differences among children. Differences among verbs seem more idiosyncratic. Across all of the experimental studies of verb comprehension, few verbs are reliably understood by all children at a given age. As discussed in more detail by Naigles and Hoff (2006), such a cross-study inconsistency is symptomatic of a deeper issue with respect to early verb acquisition: the order in which children acquire particular verbs seems quite idiosyncratic, probably because children's input is idiosyncratic in the particular verbs it illustrates. Diary studies of production overcome this problem by casting a wide net to capture whatever verbs children learn. Analyses of individual children's developing verb uses also avoids assuming that there is a single course of verb development that can be found by studying data averaged across many children.

LEARNING VERB GRAMMAR

Theories of Early Verb Grammar

When verbs first appear in children's speech, they frequently appear in multiword utterances. The nature of the representations that underlie these first combinations of verbs with other words is a point of conflict among accounts of verb development and is also a central issue with respect to the broader question of how children achieve grammar. The view that has been standard in linguistics for decades is that word combination reflects the operation of a productive grammar that operates over abstract categories, which are independent of function or meaning (Chomsky, 1975, 1981, 1995; Crain & Lillo-Martin, 1999). Children combine their verbs because they know something about the syntactic properties of items in the category VERB (e.g., that all verbs in English require subjects, that some verbs require objects while others prohibit them, that many verbs appear with the "-ing" suffix to indicate ongoing activity) and they recognize the verbs in their lexicons as belonging to that category.

6

An alternative view, consistent with the child as a conservative learner who stays close to experience in production, is that children's combinations of verbs with other lexical items reflect the operation of lexically specific rules. According to this view, there is no abstract category VERB to which individual verbs belong (Tomasello, 1992, 2000, 2006). A child who has discovered that one verb can appear with a subject, direct object, "-ing" suffix, and/or prepositional phrase thus will have no basis for extending this discovery to other verbs at the same point in time (MacWhinney, 2004; Pine, Lieven, & Rowland, 1998; Theakston, Lieven, Pine, & Rowland, 2001). Most of these latter theorists agree that children eventually attain an abstract grammar, although they may still disagree with formal generative accounts concerning the exact nature or level of the abstraction. Thus, these theories need to include an account of how children's verbs and verb combinations are transformed from lexically based to abstract.

Evidence From the Study of Verb Learning

Evidence for Early Abstract Grammar

The claim has been made from several quarters that structural regularities in children's earliest combinations are evidence that children have abstract grammatical categories, including the category VERB (Borer & Wexler, 1987; Fisher & Gleitman, 2002; Gleitman & Newport, 1995; Pinker, 1984; Valian, 1990). Two kinds of evidence from comprehension studies also argue that young children know more about verb syntax than just the combinatorial possibilities of individual verbs. First, 21–28-month-old children who have been taught a novel verb in one syntactic frame show they can distinguish that verb from another when both are presented in a new syntactic frame (Naigles et al., 2005). Second, children know a great deal about sentence frames, independent of any verb they contain, which also suggests that frames are not just represented as properties of specific verbs. For example, 1-year-old children understand the subject–verb–object (SVO) word order of simple English sentences when given noun–verb–noun (NVN) sequences with novel verbs (Gertner, Fisher, & Eisengart, 2006). That is, they infer the first noun of an NVN sequence (e.g., "The duck gorps the bunny") is the agent of a novel action presented in a video clip. Moreover, 2-year-olds map novel verbs in NVN sentences onto causative actions (in which the duck is doing something to the bunny), and they map novel verbs presented in NNV sentences (e.g., "The duck and the bunny are gorping") onto noncausative actions (in which the duck and bunny are doing the same independent action, side by side)—again, as evidenced by the scenes they prefer to look at when such sentences with novel verbs are presented to them (Fisher, 1996; Hirsh-Pasek, Golinkoff, & Naigles, 1996; Naigles, 1990).

Further evidence that 2-year-olds represent meanings with frames and not just with lexical items comes from studies in which children are asked to act out sentences in which frame meaning and verb meaning conflict. So, given a sentence such as *the zebra goes the lion*, 2-year-olds infer a causative meaning from the NVN frame and have the zebra do something to the lion, but given a sentence such as *the zebra brings*), children infer a noncausative meaning (despite the causative meaning of *bring*) and have the zebra do something without any affected object (Naigles, Gleitman, & Gleitman, 1993). Finally, Naigles et al. (2005) also found that 21- and 28-month-olds could recognize novel verbs in unattested frames; that is, verbs taught in the transitive frame were reliably recognized when presented in an intransitive frame (see also Fernandes, Marcus, Di Nubila, & Vouloumanos, 2006).

These findings, taken together, support the existence of abstract-level transitive and intransitive frames in the linguistic knowledge bases of 1- and 2-year-old English learners. They do not, however, indicate the range of flexibility (i.e., how much or how early) that toddlers are capable of, nor do they tell us about the level of flexibility that children will muster in their own productions. And yet production matters, because production flexibility is the hallmark of adult language use in all theories (Chomsky, 1975; H. Clark, 1996; Pinker, 1994; Tomasello, 2000). We therefore turn to data from children's production of verbs and sentences.

Evidence for Early Lexically Specific Grammar

In contrast to the evidence from comprehension studies that young children possess abstract grammatical knowledge that allows them to in-terpret verbs flexibly, the evidence from studies of production yields a pic-ture of limited flexibility, which has been taken as support for the view that early grammar is lexically based. Tomasello (1992) argued for this view on the basis of his diary records of his daughter's verb uses during her 2nd year of life. This 1-year-old child tended to use her verbs in only one construc-tion type per verb (i.e., one frame); for example, she might say "Mommy break" and "Daddy break" but not "Break cup" or "Break with stick." Fewer than one third of her verbs were used in more than two construction types over the span of her 2nd year. Likewise, the child was uneven in her production of lexical subjects and morphological markers; lexical subjects were produced consistently for some verbs (*take, get*) but not for others (*put*), and some verbs received tense markers, others aspect markers, but very few received both (see also Tomasello, 2000). Studies involving more children have also found limited productivity of early verb use (e.g., Matthews, Lieven, Theakston, & Tomasello, 2005; Pine et al., 1998; Theakston,

Lieven, & Tomasello, 2003; Theakston et al., 2001). These latter findings are not independent, however, because much of these data come from the same Manchester corpus, in which 12 children's spontaneous speech during lunchtime and toy play was recorded monthly for 6 months, beginning at the onset of multiword speech.

Across all of these studies, productivity was "counted" if a child used a given frame or morphological marker with different lexical items and/or the same lexical item in different frames or with different morphological markers. Using these criteria, these researchers have found evidence for productivity of the marker of the present progressive (-*ing*), but not for the past tense, third person singular, auxiliaries, SV, or SVO frames (see also Armon-Lotem & Berman, 2003, for similar findings from Hebrew learners). Also arguing for limited productivity, Theakston, Lieven, Pine, and Rowland (2004) discovered, when analyzing children's uses of *go*, that different forms were used in nonoverlapping contexts, suggesting different forms were associated with different meanings (i.e., *The train goes choo-choo* and *Mommy went to work*) rather than productive use of one meaning (i.e., *Mommy went to work/outside* and *Johnny likes going to the park*). The flexibility that was observed (with individual verbs and/or children) seemed attributable to imitations of varied uses in the maternal input (Theakston et al., 2001), or emerged piecemeal via one-word additions or deletions to previously produced phrases (e.g., from "I want a W" to "I want a book") (Lieven, 2006; Lieven, Behrens, Speares, & Tomasello, 2003). Finally, McClure, Pine, and Lieven (2006) compared the children's verb use at Stage I (MLU < 2.0) and Stage II (MLU between 2.0 and 2.5), finding that "old" verbs (those used at both stages) appeared in more complex structures than "new" verbs (those first observed at Stage II). Thus, it appears from these data that children's ability to use verbs in more complex structures is related to the length of time they have known the verbs and hence children's ability to use a verb in a given frame is not predictable from their use of other verbs in that frame, as might be expected if all verbs are treated as full members of the same abstract category .

Experimental studies of elicited speech have yielded similar findings: Children under 2.5 years who were taught novel verbs for novel actions rarely if ever used a just-learned verb in an unattested frame. That is, children taught a verb in the intransitive (e.g., *Ernie chams*) did not use it spontaneously in the transitive (*Ernie is chamming Bert*) (Akhtar & Tomasello, 1997; Brooks & Tomasello, 1999; Olguin & Tomasello, 1993; see Tomasello, 2000, for a summary, also, Naigles, 2002, 2003; Tomasello & Akhtar, 2003). Only older children, and especially those taught novel verbs in frames distributed over several sessions rather than massed in a single session, were able to use the novel verbs in unattested frames (Ambridge, Theakston, Lieven, & Tomasello, 2006).

9

In sum, research on children's early productive verb use (i.e., before 2.5 years) has found that young verb users do not routinely use their verbs in multiple grammatical forms and sentence frames, nor do they routinely use grammatical forms and frames with multiple verbs. The research that yields these findings is limited, however, by four major factors:

First, Tomasello's (1992) verb diary study included only one participant; thus, the extent to which those findings can be generalized is unknown (but will be investigated in the current research).

Second and more importantly, studies with larger sample sizes have only sampled the children's speech, with the consequence that the full flexibility of verb use is unlikely to have been represented in the speech available for analysis. Given that the recorded utterances comprise just a very small portion of the speech the child produced, it seems unwarranted to draw conclusions about those words, morphemes, and syntactic constructions that did not appear in the sample because these could have been used by the child while not being recorded (Demuth, 1996; Naigles, 2002; Stromswold, 1996; Tomasello & Stahl, 2004). Many of the speech samples were also restricted in context (i.e., recording the same setting at each visit, Lieven, 2006; Lieven et al., 2003) as well as time, thereby limiting the objects, actions, and people that could be the topics of conversation. For example, if a child is consistently recorded during breakfast and after-breakfast free play, then the conversation is likely to involve expressions of wanting things (food, toys) and suggestions for action ("let's . . . "). Over time, the same types of conversations would recur, with the child adding on more words as, perhaps, her vocabulary grows and her working memory/production system continues to develop (Lieven et al., 2003). But *very* novel utterances would not necessarily be seen, unless the child is also recorded at *different* times of the day and different settings. As Naigles and Hoff (2006) have reported, the verbs used by mothers, at least, vary dramatically according to setting; it is unlikely that children's verb use would be any different. And given that mothers do not even always use every word and frame flexibly in their sampled speech (Lieven et al., 2003; Theakston et al., 2003), when they, unarguably, have full command of productive grammar, it is unwarranted to attribute children's lack of flexibility to a less-than-full command of the same. Because children talk less than their mothers, they would, in fact, demonstrate less flexibility in their sampled speech by base rates alone.

Third, the "conservative-child" argument assumes that when children's verb uses omit a subject or object, such omissions reflect limited grammatical knowledge. However, Matthews, Lieven, Theakston, and Tomasello (2006) and Valian, Prasada, and Scarpa (2006) have recently demonstrated that toddlers' production of subjects and objects in elicited production tasks varies systematically according to discourse and processing constraints (e.g., toddlers use fewer full NPs when the referents of those NPs have just been labeled, and they imitate full NPs less frequently when these are part of longer target sentences). Allen and Schroder (2003) have also found that toddlers' spontaneous production of lexical subjects and objects is highly constrained by the discourse context. Because the linguistic and discourse context affects whether or not children produce NPs, children's production of a given verb with only one NP is not good evidence that the child thinks that verb has only one argument. Such utterances may reflect *pragmatic* sensitivity on the child's part, rather than limited grammatical knowledge.

Fourth, the import of the experimental findings that suggested limited grammatical flexibility associated with verbs is itself limited by the fact that most of the types of frame productivity that have been tested have involved meaning changes as well as frame changes. That is, the use of specific verbs in specific frames is partially governed by each verb's semantics; for example, causative verbs do not usually appear in intransitive frames, motion verbs do not appear with sentence complements, and so on (Fisher, Gleitman, & Gleitman, 1991; Jackendoff, 1983, 1990; Levin, 1993). As described in more detail by Naigles (2002), children's reluctance to use a novel verb in an unattested frame could be traced to their uncertainty about whether the verb's meaning was suitable for the frame, rather than their not knowing the frame independently of the verbs already used in it (see also Tomasello & Akhtar, 2003; Naigles, 2003).

Thus, even when children's verb uses truly show less grammatical flexibility than a fully productive system would support, there are two possible interpretations: One is that toddlers' knowledge of simple sentence frames is abstract, but they use a limited range of grammatical options in their verb uses because they use their verbs to express only a limited range of meanings. On this account, it is the limited understanding of verb meaning that underlies the limited grammatical flexibility of verb use. An alternative interpretation is that toddlers' initial knowledge of simple sentence frames is indeed lexically specific. For example, a child might know both *drop* and *move* can be causal, but having heard *move* but not *drop* in the transitive frame thus far, he only produces *move* in this frame. On this account, it is limited syntactic knowledge causes that initial conservative verb use.

A Mechanism of Transition From Lexically Specific to Abstract Grammar

Thus far we have been considering the evidence regarding when children have an abstract grammar that allows newly acquired verbs to be recognized as instances of a category and freely combined with inflectional morphemes and syntactic frames. Another question, which is crucial to a full account of verb development, is how the child achieves such a grammatical system. According to the strongest generativist position, the grammatical categories themselves, and the configurations they could possibly appear in, are innate (Chomsky, 1975, 1995; Crain & Lillo-Martin, 1999). At least some aspects of this innateness may be rendered unnecessary if it could be shown that children discover grammatical categories and/or language-specific syntactic configurations from their input before combinatorial speech begins, and studies of infant learning of language structure make this a plausible suggestion (see Brent, 1993; Gerken, 2007; Gomez 2002; Mintz, 2003; Naigles, 2002). However, rejection of such innateness is also a central tenet of positions that attribute little syntactic competence to young children. According to the lexically specific grammar view, children begin to combine verbs with other words *before* they have achieved grammatical categories and/or abstract syntactic patterning (MacWhinney, 2004; Tomasello, 2000). Thus, a full account consistent with an early lexically specific grammar requires an account of how children move from that state to having an abstract grammar.

A set of influential suggestions revolves around the idea that a subset of verbs, verbs that are frequent in input and have general meanings, called "light" verbs, serve as the child's entry into abstract grammatical forms and their meanings (Chenu & Jisa, 2006; E. Clark, 1987, 1996, 2003; Goldberg, 1999; Goldberg et al., 2004; Goodman & Sethuraman, 2006; Ninio, 1999; but see Campbell & Tomasello, 2001). This proposal that light verbs provide entry into the grammatical system comes in several forms, three of which we summarize here.

The proposal of Goldberg and her colleagues (2004) focuses on the *meanings* of the frames or constructions to be acquired and relies on both frequency and general semantic attributes of light verbs. Essentially, Goldberg hypothesizes that children's hearings of the high-frequency verb *go* followed by a prepositional phrase or locative—*go to the store, go around the table, go outside*—(+PP frame or verb+locative [VL] construction) and the high-frequency verb *put* in the +NP PP frame (or V+object+L [VOL] construction)—*put the bowl on the table, put the bowl there*—enables them to associate the general meanings of *go* and *put* (inchoative motion and caused motion, respectively) with the VL and VOL frames (Goldberg, 1999; Goldberg & Casenhiser, 2006; Goldberg et al., 2003; Goodman & Sethuraman, 2006). Thus, the children's meanings of the light verbs are "transferred" to the meanings of the frames or constructions that they typically appear in so that the light verbs enable the frames' meanings to be acquired (see Casenhiser & Goldberg, 2005, for supporting evidence from grade schoolers' acquisition of nonsense verbs). This theory does not predict, though, that light verbs should be the first verbs to appear in child speech in a given frame—light verbs do their work during comprehension. They are considered to be the engine of learning about construction meaning, but not necessarily the first consequence of this learning observable in children's productions (Goldberg et al., 2004). And the theory is silent on how the frame or construction forms, themselves, are acquired.

12

A second version of the light verb proposal does address children's acquisition of syntactic form, hypothesizing that each frame is first learned with a single light verb, and only later extended to other verbs (E. Clark, 1987, 2003; Chenu & Jisa, 2006; Ninio, 1999). These researchers' rationale for this special role for light verbs is similar to Goldberg's: Light verbs most closely encode the meanings of specific frames or constructions (i.e., *go* is the canonical motion verb, exemplifying the +PP frame, *make* is the canonical causal/acting on verb, exemplifying the transitive frame, and *put* is the canonical transfer verb, exemplifying the +NP PP frame). The specific hypothesis is that light verbs should be the first to appear in a given frame because the form–meaning relation is so transparent. *Go* is learned to be used with a PP or L because *go* transparently encodes motion, so any accompanying arguments must involve locatives (*go home/to the store*). Then children's use of *go* with a variety of PPs or Ls enables them to abstract a more general +PP or VL frame, which they can then transfer for use with more specific verbs such as *run* and (eventually) *cry*. The idea is that the first verb used in a given frame is that frame's *pathbreaker* (Ninio, 1999), which, by virtue of its general meaning, facilitates children's formalization of that frame and thus their use of other verbs in that frame.

Further predictions from this light-verbs-as-pathbreakers hypothesis include that light verbs should be used in ways both more grammatically complex and more grammatically flexible than heavy verbs learned at the same time (E. Clark, 1987; Ninio, 1999; Theakston et al., 2004). Both of these predictions follow from the semantic generality of light verbs: Because verbs such as *go* and *put* can apply to any type of inchoative or caused motion (respectively), specifics about which entities are participating in these motions are not always recoverable from the context. For example, *eat* usually only involves eatable things, whereas *put* can involve a wide range of things put, and *run* usually only involves animates engaged in forward horizontal motion, whereas *go* can involve either animates or inanimates engaged in motion in any direction. Thus, in response to the communicative pressure to be as clear as possible (Grice, 1989), *go* and *put* should be more likely to appear with overt arguments than *run* and *eat*. Furthermore, semantically general verbs are more syntactically diverse in the adult language (Levin, 1993; Naigles & Hoff-Ginsberg, 1995, 1998) because their general meanings allow them to fit into a wider variety of sentence frames (Snedeker & Gleitman, 2004). For example, *bring* can be used both with and without a PP, depending on whether the speaker chooses to focus on the action or goal of bringing (e.g., *What's Molly doing? She's bringing the pizza/Where is Molly going so quickly? She's bringing the pizza to the library*), and *go* but not *run* can be used with a preverbal P (e.g., *Up you go!* but not *Up you run!*—for most speakers).

The current evidence for light verbs as "pathbreakers" to an abstract grammar is mixed: Ninio (1999) and Chenu and Jisa (2006) report, based

13

on spontaneous speech samples from children learning Hebrew, English, and French, that many children first used a given frame with only one verb; moreover, they took from 43 days (Ninio, 1999) to several months (Chenu & Jisa, 2006) to produce that frame with a second verb. However, Ninio (1999) and Theakston et al. (2004) have also found that these pathbreaking verbs were not always light verbs. Ninio (1999) has reconciled this divergent finding with the light-verbs-as-pathbreakers hypothesis by maintaining the "pathbreaking" notion but broadening what counts as a light or "canonical" verb for a given frame. In particular, *want*, a frequent first verb in SVO frames, is included as a canonical/general transitive verb even though it does not encode "highly transitive" senses such as change of state or position (i.e., Hopper & Thompson, 1980; Thompson & Hopper, 2001). Theakston et al. (2004) also point out, though, that because semantic generality and input frequency are confounded, it is not clear which factor contributes more heavily to children's acquisition of grammatical forms. They found no difference between light and heavy verbs in their numbers of different frames, percent of utterances with subjects, nor percent of utterances with objects, once input frequency was partialled out. Apart from the mixed nature of the evidence, a problem with evaluating the light-verbs-as-pathbreakers hypothesis is that all of the relevant data thus far have been drawn from samples of spontaneous speech of limited duration and limited contextual range; such findings are tenuous for the sampling reasons discussed earlier. Moreover, almost all of the research thus far has investigated the behavior of light verbs as a class, even though the light-verbs-as-pathbreakers proposal really targets several individual light verbs as pathbreakers for specific frames (i.e., *go* for the VL/+PP frame and *put* for the VOL/+NP PP frame), and furthermore, the particular light verb serving the pathbreaker function could be different for different children.

Snedeker and Gleitman (2004) propose that light verbs are the products of syntactic acquisition rather than its engines. They argue that light verbs do not have specific meanings that could be inferred from observation as, for example, the meaning of *eat* could be inferred from observing eaters. Thus, light verbs are more dependent on syntax for their acquisition than heavy verbs. This argument receives support in findings from their Human Simulation Paradigm (Gillette, Gleitman, Gleitman, & Lederer, 1999), in which adults are given video clips of mother–child conversation and told to guess what verb is produced when a tone sounds. Light verbs (e.g., *go* and *put*) required *more* syntactic information to be accurately guessed than the "heavy" verbs (e.g., *run* and *throw*) (Snedeker & Gleitman, 2004). One prediction for children's speech that follows from this view is that light verbs should appear less frequently than heavy verbs in verb-only phrases and more frequently with sentence frames because the light verbs should be acquired *after* (and because of) the sentence frames.

Questions to Be Addressed Regarding Children's Acquisition of Verb Grammar

Understanding when and how children become grammatically productive users of their verb lexicons is central to understanding when and how children become adult-like language users. The foregoing review of the existing literature reveals the following questions about early verb productivity, and thus about the flexibility of children's early verb use, that form a focus of the present study:

1. How early in the course of verb learning does grammatical productivity—or at least flexibility—emerge? Prior studies have demonstrated that 1- and 2-year-old children can understand novel verbs in SVO frames and distinguish novel verbs in transitive versus intransitive frames (Gertner et al., 2006; Naigles, 1998). Still, the existing studies of children of that age have not found good evidence of such productivity in their spontaneous speech (Pine et al., 1998; Theakston et al., 2003). A big gap in the literature, which the current study was designed to fill, results from the fact that no studies have tracked several children's productivity in spontaneous speech in a way that includes *all* uses of their *very first* verbs.

It is important to delineate, though, how much of the gap in the literature the current study can fill. The productivity that is the hallmark of human language is the capacity to produce and understand utterances one has never heard before. The most unambiguous evidence of this capacity in spontaneous speech is the production of errors—utterances such as "don't fall that on me" (Bowerman, 1973)—because the child is not likely to ever have heard such an utterance. Comprehension studies can elicit unambiguous evidence that children understand utterances they have never heard by testing children with experimenter-created utterances using nonsense words, such as "the duck is gorping the bunny" (Naigles, 1990). Because our study relies on children's spontaneous productions of verbs in their conventional uses, without a comprehensive analysis of their input, we will not be able to make claims about this level of productivity. However, many researchers have looked at spontaneous speech for evidence of productivity by taking flexibility of use as indicating, albeit indirectly, underlying productivity (Ingram, 1989; Shirai, 1998; Tomasello, 1992). If a child can use a single verb in multiple frames or a single frame with multiple verbs, this suggests a productive system at work. Without knowing the child's input, it is always possible that these multiple uses are all input-based rather than generated anew, but the greater the flexibility the child demonstrates the less plausible that account becomes. Using a metric that the production of three to five verbs in a given frame displays some amount of productivity, various researchers have reported productivity in 1- to 2-year-old children with frames such as V-ing, SV, VO, SVO (Ingram, 1981; Pine et al., 1998; Shirai, 1998; Tomasello, 1992). In the present study we similarly adopt the three-verbs-per-frame and five-verbs-per-frame measures of productivity as less unambiguous but still valuable indicators of the children's ability to use their frames flexibly and independently of specific verbs.

In this study we also introduce several additional measures, which we argue index the productivity of the underlying system. We investigate children's ability to use their verbs with multiple frames, which we term grammatical *flexibility*. That is, Tomasello (1992) claimed that Travis's "inability" to use *break* with both Ss and Os illustrated limitations in her grammar; therefore, we investigate the extent to which our child subjects did use their verbs—within the first 10 instances—with the appropriate grammatical arguments and morphemes. We also investigate the degree to which these latter two types of flexibility are related to each other: Does it automatically follow that a child who uses *eat* with both Ss and Os might also use the SV or VO frame with multiple verbs?

2. If children do not initially have adult-like productivity, what is the process by which they achieve it? Several studies have found evidence of "pathbreaking" verbs in children's speech; that is, verbs that seem to lead the way to productivity with a given frame. The view that some verbs serve as the child's entry into abstract grammatical frames suggests that there should be differences among verbs when they first appear in children's speech in the degree to which they show grammatical flexibility and complexity. Moreover, whether the same verbs serve this function for all children, and whether light verbs, specifically, serve this function and are the earliest verbs to show grammatical productivity, are all questions still unanswered, which will be addressed in the current study. Because our onset of data collection was verb driven rather than frame driven, though, we will not address whether the children's first uses of a frame occur with light verbs but rather whether children's first uses of light verbs demonstrate more grammatical flexibility than their first uses of heavy verbs.

Relations Among Different Aspects of Early Verb Growth and Use

Some of the contrasting theoretical positions on the nature of early verb development yield empirically distinguishable predictions regarding the relations between flexibility of meaning and flexibility of grammar as they develop and the relation of the development of both types of flexibility of verb use to growth in the verb lexicon. According to generativist theories, the grammar is formal, abstract, and autonomous (Chomsky, 1995, 1998; Borer & Wexler, 1987). Therefore, acquisition of a verb lexicon, development of semantically flexible uses of those verbs, and development of grammatically flexible uses of those verbs should all be unrelated, aside from the obvious necessity that children who have more words at their command would be able to produce longer sentences.

Other theories predict there will be relations among lexical size, semantic flexibility, and grammatical flexibility. There are many arguments that language development is the product of domain-general learning mechanisms (Bates, Bretherton, & Synder, 1988; Elman, et al., 1996; Saffran & Thiessen, 2007), and these predict that all the measures of development—the number of verbs acquired and the semantic and grammatical flexibility with which they are used—should be at least loosely related. A stronger prediction of relatedness comes from the view that grammar emerges from the lexicon. According to this view lexical development must precede grammatical development, because a certain threshold or "critical mass" of vocabulary must be achieved before grammatical patterns can be abstracted (Childers & Tomasello, 2006; Marchman & Bates, 1994; Plunkett & Marchman, 1993; Robinson & Mervis, 1998) and, in some accounts, grammar continues to develop as a result of reorganizational processes caused by a growing lexicon (Conboy & Thal, 2006). These views yield the prediction that grammatical flexibility should be positively correlated with children's number of verbs. The syntactic bootstrapping hypothesis also yields the prediction that the size of the verb lexicon should be positively related to the flexibility and overall grammatical complexity of verb use because grammar is the source of meaning-relevant information that contributes to learning verbs. Both the shared mechanism and syntactic bootstrapping hypotheses predict a positive relation between semantic and syntactic flexibility of verb use. The shared-mechanism hypothesis predicts that the relation between semantic and syntactic flexibility should be across children—children who show more semantic flexibility should also show more grammatical flexibility. The syntactic bootstrapping hypothesis additionally predicts a relation between grammatical flexibility and semantic flexibility across verbs, because it is knowledge of a particular verb's structural possibilities that supports its semantically flexible use.

Numerous studies support the conclusion that the size of children's vocabularies and the grammatical complexity of their speech are related (Bates & Goodman, 1999; Caselli, Casadio, & Bates, 1999; Jackson-Maldonado, Thal, Marchman, Bates, & Guitierrez-Clellen, 1993; Maital, Dromi, Sagi, & Bornstein, 2000; Marchman & Bates, 1994; Marchman, Martinez-Sussman, & Dale, 2004; Ogura, Yamashita, Murase, & Dale, 1993; Robinson & Mervis, 1998). More specific predictions are less well supported. The claim that lexical development initially proceeds ahead of

17

grammatical development and that grammatical development is paced by the preceding lexical development is largely based on studies that used the Words and Sentences form of the MacArthur–Bates Communicative Development Inventory (CDI; Fenson et al., 1994). The CDI includes a checklist of over 600 words plus a section in which pairs of phrases (one closer to the adult form than the other; e.g., *two shoe* vs. *two shoes*) are listed; the parent checks off the phrase that is closer to the child's current level of speech. These studies have reported a curvilinear relation in which children who produce more words are also reported to produce more complex grammatical forms, with smaller changes in grammatical complexity associated with early increments in vocabulary size and larger changes in grammatical complexity associated with later, equal-sized increments in vocabulary.

There are, however, a variety of reasons to think that the statistical relations observed in these data do not necessarily imply that grammatical development depends on lexical development. First, measurement issues abound. In the studies of spontaneous speech (Bates et al., 1988; Robinson & Mervis, 1998), MLU was used as the measure of grammatical development, and MLU is not a pure measure of grammar apart from the size of the lexicon. Indeed, as Rollins, Snow, and Willett (1996) reported in their study of children's sampled spontaneous speech, the MLU growth between 14 and 32 months for a substantial percent of the children was accounted for by growth in content words alone, not in morphological or other grammatical items. Thus, a relation between vocabulary size and MLU does not necessarily reflect a relation between lexical development and grammatical development. Rather it may reflect the greater expressive possibilities afforded by a larger vocabulary.

Two problems particularly apply to the many studies that have used the CDI. Because the measures of vocabulary and grammar are taken from the same parental report instrument, they may share the same parental bias. Most critically, the ordering interpretation of the observed curvilinear relation between the vocabulary and grammar measures depends on the assumption that the measurement of vocabulary and the measurement of grammar were equally sensitive measures of change across the range of development studies. Dixon and Marchman (2007) have argued that this assumption is demonstrably false. They performed nonlinear function analyses which revealed that, while the vocabulary section of the CDI mapped linearly onto the underlying lexicon (i.e., increases in vocabulary are uniformly related to increases in underlying lexicon), the grammar section mapped nonuniformly, such that early changes in grammar are underrepresented in the CDI, relative to later ones. The curvilinear relation observed between lexical development and grammatical development is, they argue, an artifact of the differences between the measures of lexical and grammatical development in their sensitivity to early growth.

Finally, to the extent that the observed (linear) correlations are real, they still do not reveal the source or direction of causality. The possibility that vocabulary knowledge supports the induction of grammar and the alternate possibility that grammatical knowledge supports the induction of word meaning are different language learning mechanisms that would both be reflected in a correlation between vocabulary size and grammatical usage. Also, neither the CDI nor the previous analyses of spontaneous word use have assessed what children know about the words they use—only that they use them—nor have they assessed children's use of argument structure or sentence frames—only that words appear in combination and some inflections are present. Thus, to the degree that vocabulary knowledge may support the achievement of grammatical understandings, it is not clear just what about vocabulary knowledge is doing the supporting and what about grammatical understanding is being supported.

Previous studies have not examined the semantic flexibility of children's verb use, and thus have not captured possible differences among children and among verbs in what children know about the meanings of the verbs they use. A revised version of the grammar-from-lexicon hypothesis might suggest that children who know *more about* the words that they use (i.e., are more flexible with them), as opposed to knowing more words, might be able to achieve grammar or productivity sooner. Some support for this revised version comes from an experimental study that assessed toddlers' extendability of verbs' grammatical form as well as their extendability of the verbs across situations (Naigles et al., 2005). As described earlier, the 21-month-olds in this study were shown to be able to recognize verb–referent pairings, which had been taught in a playroom setting, when they were presented on video, thus demonstrating one form of extendability. Moreover, the children were also shown to recognize the verb–referent pairings that had been taught in the transitive frame but tested in the intransitive frame (e.g., children were taught *you're gorping the ball* and tested on *the ball is gorping*). Strikingly, it was the children who could distinguish (i.e., had learned) the verb–referent pairings in the transitive who were more likely to be able to extend them to the intransitive. These findings suggest there is some threshold of semantic learning required before grammatical flexibility could be demonstrated.

The current study was designed to investigate these issues in more detail, asking whether children who use verbs more flexibly in terms of their semantics also use them more flexibly in terms of their grammar. We will also examine the relations among types of flexibility as a characteristic of verbs. That is, we ask whether verbs that are used more flexibly in terms of their semantics also more likely to be used more flexibly in terms of their grammar.

THE PRESENT STUDY

The foregoing review of the theoretical and empirical literature on children's acquisition of verbs makes it clear that a central and unanswered question is when in the course of verb development children extend their verbs beyond the functions, referents, and morphosyntactic structures in which they have heard them used. The question is as yet unanswered because the research methodologies that have been brought to bear are limited in several ways. Sampling naturalistic parent/child interactions (e.g., collecting 3 hours of data per week for 4 months) is likely to miss situation-specific language use. Children use verbs in particular contexts that may not be recorded, such as *washing* in the bathtub, *splashing* in the pool, *sleeping* at night, and *riding* in the shopping cart at the grocery store (Naigles & Hoff, 2006; Naigles & Hoff-Ginsberg, 1998). Sampling also does not capture the full range of uses to which children put the verbs they use, thus rendering questions about the scope of meanings and forms of verb use unanswerable. Diary studies conducted with one child (e.g., Dromi, 1987; Mervis, 1987; Tomasello, 1992) may solve the sampling problems but at the cost of making it impossible to untangle evidence of processes common to all children from uses that are idiosyncratic to the single child under study.

An ideal data set for addressing the issue of when and to what degree children go beyond their input would include a record of all of the verb uses of many children—in addition to a record of all of those children's verb input. If, however, we make the assumption that verbs that are used in a variety of different ways are more likely to reflect productive and extended use than verbs that are used in only a single way, then we can begin to address some of these as yet unanswered questions with a record of children's verb uses that does not include their input (e.g., E. Clark, 2003; Ingram, 1981; Shirai, 1998)—provided the record overcomes the sampling issues discussed above.

In this study, we overcome many of the sampling issues that limit the utility of the existing evidence by returning to the diary method for capturing children's earliest uses of verbs, incorporating in the method the positive attributes of a diverse set of previous diary studies (e.g., E. Clark, 1993; Dromi, 1987; Harris et al., 1988; Robinson & Mervis, 1998; Tomasello, 1992). We included more than a single child, asking the parent participants to record their children's uses of only 34 common verbs and only the first 10 uses of those verbs. In this way, we were able to track early changes in verb use without exhausting our parent participants' capabilities. We targeted 34 of the most common verbs produced by children early in language acquisition (Goldin-Meadow, Seligman, & Gelman, 1976; Marchman & Bates, 1994; Tomasello, 1992; Tomasello & Kruger, 1992). In the next chapter we present the method in detail. In the results chapters that follow the method, we present the description of early verb development that these data suggest, and we address the questions we have outlined with respect to the pragmatic, semantic, and grammatical nature of children's first verb uses. In a concluding chapter we consider what the data imply with respect to the nature of children's early linguistic understandings.

II. PRESENTING THE DIARY METHOD

PARTICIPANTS

The data in the present study come from diary records kept by eight mothers of their children's first 10 spontaneous uses of 34 common verbs. A total of 18 mothers initially agreed to participate, but 9 mothers withdrew from the study before having collected enough data for analysis (i.e., at least 10 uses each of 10 different verbs). For five of these mothers, their reason for withdrawing was that their child (always a boy) was not talking at all, and they planned to bring the child to clinical services for evaluation and treatment. The other mothers who withdrew gave the reason that their child was talking so much that they found they could not record or make note of every relevant utterance their child produced, and so they could not keep the diary accurately. One additional mother collected data for over a year from her child and completed the diary for a total of 31 verbs. However, after the data from seven verbs were collected, she lapsed in her diary keeping for 6 months. Given this lapse, we could not be certain that the data from the last 24 verbs really reflected the child's first 10 uses of these verbs, and this child's data were not analyzed further.

At the onset of the study, the children (5 girls and 3 boys) ranged in age from 15 to 19 months; all were European American. Detailed questioning of the mothers established that none of the children had yet produced any verbs; this was supported by the absence of any spontaneous verbs in the 20-min speech sample collected during the experimenter's first visit. The children's spontaneously produced word types during this speech sample were tabulated; on average, the children produced 25.12 different words ($SD = 11.47$). At the first visit, the mothers were asked to fill a questionnaire concerning the child's siblings, the parents' education and occupation, and the child's television and reading habits. Three of the children had older siblings ($M = 5$ years, $SD = 3$ years); one also had a younger sibling (3 months of age). All but one of the parents (mothers and fathers) had attended college for at least a year (M [mothers] $= 3.33$ years, $SD = 1.97$; M [fathers] $= 4.0$ years, $SD = 2.28$). Their occupations were generally middle class (the fathers included an accountant, several engineers, an insurance executive, a landscaper, and a computer manager; the mothers had previously been accountants, teachers, and bookkeepers). All of the children were cared for at home by their mothers. The eight children watched an average of 9.83 hr of television per week ($SD = 7.54$) and were read to for an average of 11.08 hr per week ($SD = 7.67$), according to the maternal report.

MATERIALS

Each mother was provided with a bound diary with 34 individual pages. On each page was listed a different verb with 10 rows for recording the first 10 instances of that verb's use. The 34 verbs were chosen from prior data sets of the children's spontaneous verb use (Goldin-Meadow et al., 1976; Marchman & Bates, 1994; Tomasello, 1992; Tomasello & Kruger, 1992); these are all words that would be used as verbs in the adult language. They included 8 *light* verbs, which have more general meanings (H. Clark, 1996; Goldberg, 1999), and 26 *heavy* verbs, which had narrower meanings. Nine of the 34 were obligatorily transitive, 9 were obligatorily intransitive, and 16 were alternating verbs (i.e., they can appear in both transitive and intransitive frames). They are listed, by category, in Table 1. In the blank

TABLE 1

LIST OF 34 COMMON VERBS

	Transitive	Intransitive	Alternating
Light verbs	bring	come	
	give	go	
	put	look	
	take		
	want		
Heavy verbs	hold	clap	bite
	like	cry	cut
	need	fall	drop
	see	run	eat
		sit	jump
		walk	kiss
		wave	lay
			move
			open
			pull
			push
			roll
			stop
			throw
			wash

TABLE 2

Diary Page

	University of Connecticut/Florida Atlantic University First Verbs Study Child's Name___Heather___			Record of first ten uses of: Birthdate___		PULL
	Date	Record of complete utterance	Was utterance a command or description?	For commands, who or what is command addressed to? For descriptions, who or what is doing the verb action?	Who or what is receiving the verb action?	Other comments
1st	10/2	Pull	Command	Mommy	Chair	
2nd	10/3	Pull	Command	Mommy	Wagon	
3rd	12/5	I pulling	Description	Heather	Car with handle	
4th	12/8	Uncle, pull	Command	Uncle	Sled	
5th	12/8	Pulling	Command	Uncle	Sled	
6th	12/8	Auntie, pull	Command	Aunt	Sled	
7th	12/8	Auntie, pull	Command	Aunt	Sled	
8th	1/3	Mommy, pull me	Command	Mommy	Cart	
9th	1/13	I pull that	Description	Heather	Blanket	
10th	1/13	I pull this	Description	Heather	Blanket	

diary, space was provided to record the complete utterance, the date, pragmatic function (i.e., command or description), and addressee of the utterance, as well as the actor and the affected object (when relevant) of the verb's action. A sample diary page is reproduced in Table 2.

PROCEDURE

Parents with children between 15 and 19 months of age were found by searching back issues of the birth announcements of the local newspaper. Letters describing the study were sent, followed by phone calls requesting volunteers willing to keep detailed diaries of their child's verb development. Extensive questioning confirmed that the child had not produced any verbs at that point and that the parent would be in primary contact with the child (approximately 20 families were excluded at this point because their child had already begun producing verbs). All the volunteer parents were mothers. The researcher then visited the family to train the mother on diary keeping and to collect a 20-min spontaneous speech sample.

The training session was conducted first. The researcher explained that the goal of the study was to investigate the child's language development in detail, so that it was of crucial importance to make note of *every utterance* that (a) contained a target verb and (b) was not an immediate repetition of another person's speech. The researcher then introduced the diary and provided a separate list of the 34 target verbs. It was explained that our focus was on verbs because they were less well studied than nouns. The researcher discussed with the mother the difference between nominal and verb uses of homonyms (e.g., *bite* in "take a bite" vs. "bite this"), described several examples of verb uses in one-word and multiword utterances, and emphasized that the study was about verb uses only. The researcher then discussed each column of the diary page, giving examples of possible utterances and how they were to be entered in the diary. Specifically, the mothers were instructed on (a) what constituted commands (e.g., "When your child is trying to get you or someone else to do—or stop doing—something") and descriptions (e.g., "When your child is telling you about an object, event, or relation"), (b) what constituted an addressee ("Whom the command is directed to"), actor ("Who is doing the verb action"), and affected object ("Who or what is the patient of the verb action") when these were and were not labeled by the child, (c) recording the utterance as exactly as possible, including inflections such as "-ing," "-ed," and "-s" if heard, and (d) the use of the right-most column involving contextual notes (mothers were encouraged to add notes at all times, but especially when they were not sure about pragmatic or semantic roles). Then, the researcher emphasized how important it was for the mother to note *every utterance* using the target verbs until 10 instances had been produced and told the mother repeatedly that *every utterance* meant that the child's exact and inexact self-repetitions of any target verbs should be included, as well as new utterances with that verb, but not repetitions of other people's speech. The researcher suggested that the mother put the diary in an easily accessible place in the house and carry the diary along whenever she and the child went out. The researcher asked and noted which words the child was currently producing (in case some verbs had emerged since the phone call; none had). The researcher then described her own role, which would be to phone the family every 2 weeks until the child began producing the target verbs. Once verb production began, the researcher would phone the family every week to check how data collection was proceeding and to answer any questions the family might have. The training session ended with a discussion of the duration for data collection; each mother was asked to keep the diary for at least 3 months. The actual duration of the study varied from child to child, ranging from a minimum of 3 months to a maximum of 13 months ($M = 8.625$ months, $SD = 3.62$).

25

After the training session, the researcher asked the mother to play with her child for about 20 min so that the child's current level of speech production could be recorded. The researcher brought toys for them to play with; they could also play with their own toys and read their own books (although little book reading was conducted), doing whatever they usually did at that time of day. The researcher then started the audio recorder and left the room for 20 min, staying outside or in another part of the house. Audio recording was used instead of video recording to minimize feelings of self-consciousness and concerns about privacy.

After this initial visit, biweekly phone calls were made to each family until the child began producing the target verbs. Then, the family was called weekly, reminding the parents of the diary procedure (especially, to record *every utterance*) and answering any questions the parents might have had in filling out the diary. Mothers typically used these conversations to discuss the children's new utterances and the records thereof, describing the utterances in detail and receiving confirmation and/or instruction concerning how they were recorded. Mothers reported little difficulty with the level of detail required by the records; those who did acknowledge some difficulty were the ones who soon asked to leave the study. Table 3 displays each child's age at the onset of the study, duration of the study, and the total number of target verbs produced to the 10-instance criterion out of the 34. Only those verbs for which all 10 instances were recorded were included in any of the coding and analyses.

MEASURES

The diary records provided measures of the age at which each verb was used and the number of days elapsed from the 1st to the 10th instance of

TABLE 3

AGE AND NUMBER OF VERBS PRODUCED BY EACH CHILD

Child	Age at Onset	Length of Study	# of Verbs Produced (Out of a Possible 34)	Rate of Target Verb Growth
Carl	1;8	11 months	24	2.18/month
Carrie	1;7	7 months	30	4.42/month
Elaine	1;8	5 months	19	3.8/month
Heather	1;7	7 months	31	4.42/month
Mae	1;7	13 months	31	2.38/month
Ned	1;5	3 months	14	4.67/month
Sam	1;6	11 months	31	2.82/month
Stacey	1;4	12 months	20	1.67/month
Mean	1;6	8.625 months	24.5	3.21/month
SD	1.5	3.62	7.07	1.15

use. In addition, the following measures were taken from the diary records or coded based on the information the mothers recorded:

Pragmatic Content

Each verb use was coded as a command or description (these accounted for over 98% of all utterances), and for each command, the addressee was noted. To illustrate, in Instance 1 of Table 2, Heather says "Pull" as a command to her mother to pull a chair; in Instance 3 she says "I pulling" as a description of her own actions with the toy car. The addressee is the person to whom the utterance is directed; in Instance 1, this is the child's mother, and in Instance 4 it is her uncle.

Semantic Role

The semantic properties recorded for each verb use were the particular person or objects filling the roles entailed by each verb. For all verbs, this involved recording who or what served as the actor, agent, or experiencer of the verb. For transitive and alternating verbs, who or what served as patient or theme was also recorded. For example, when a child said "jumping" and her mother recorded the child in the actor cell, then the child was coded as the actor of the action. With regard to affected objects, an utterance of "Pull" with "chair" recorded in the affected object cell would be coded with "chair" as the affected object, whereas an utterance of "pull me" would be coded with "Heather" as the affected object. These assignments of actor and affected object were made regardless of whether the semantic roles were overtly expressed or not because the purpose of the coding was to capture the extent to which children extend these verbs to actions by multiple actors and on multiple objects. The mothers were carefully instructed on how to determine actors and affected objects when these were not overtly expressed.

Action Referent

Each instance of each verb's use was coded as the same or different from previous uses of the verb in terms of the physical action referred to. This judgment was made for uses of 28 of the 34 target verbs, based on the actor, affected object, and other notes recorded by the mother. Action referent change was not coded for four internal event verbs (*like, look, need, see, want*), and it was not coded for the verb *bring* because the specific action referred to by uses of this verb was difficult to discern from the diaries. In our first pass of coding the action content of the remaining verbs, utterance pairs of the same verb were hypothesized to refer to different actions if (a) the actors were of different species (e.g., dog running vs. child running) or kinds (e.g., child coming vs. TV show coming), (b) the affected objects were of different

27

kinds (e.g., eating rocks vs. eating an apple), sizes (e.g., washing a chair vs. washing dishes) or configurations (e.g., opening a bag vs. opening a plastic container), or (c) the situations pertained to different locations (coming downstairs vs. coming out of the house), directions (taking Legos off vs. taking a Poptart out), or activities (taking a nap vs. taking a shower). A total of 93 distinct action pairs were initially identified. These were then presented in randomized order to 11 undergraduates, who were asked to rate them on a scale of 1–7, where 1 indicated *the pairs described identical physical actions* and 7 indicated that *the pairs described completely different physical actions*. An additional 20 items were included to anchor the lower end of the scale; these included action pairs performed by similar actors to similar affected objects in similar situations. The ratings were averaged for each action pair and only those whose rating averaged 4.0 or higher ($n = 76$) were included in the final analysis (mean rating for these 76 pairs averaged 5.63, $SD = 0.84$). The complete list of action pairs and ratings can be obtained from the authors.

Grammatical Frame

The grammatical frame of each target verb use was coded from the mothers' records of the children's complete verb-containing utterance. The coded components included overt subjects, objects, morphological markers, location words, negative markers, preposition/prepositional phrases, and full subject–verb–object (SVO) frames. For example, the utterance "I drop my cracker" includes a subject "I" and an object "my cracker"; it encompasses a full SVO frame. The utterance "My fall down" includes a subject "my" and a preposition "down." The utterance "no clapping" includes the morphological marker "-ing" and the negative marker "no," and the utterance "Go there" includes the locative form "there." Vocatives (e.g., *Mommy* in *Mommy, push me*) were not counted as a grammatical frame component.

Flexibility

In order to calculate flexibility of verb use, each instance of a verb in spontaneous speech was coded as the same or changed from previous instances in terms of its pragmatics, semantics, and grammatical frame. Changes are defined below and examples are provided in Table 4.

Pragmatic Flexibility

Two types of change were counted as instances of pragmatic flexibility: changes in function and changes in addressee. A function change was coded when a child first switched from using commands to using descriptions, or

TABLE 4

FLEXIBILITY CODING

Type of Flexibility	Baseline Instance	Changed Instance
Pragmatic		
Function	Pull (Command)	I pulling (Description)
Addressee	Pull (Ad = Mommy).	Uncle, pull (Ad = uncle)
Semantic		
Actor (A)	Eating (A = daddy)	Eating (A = dog)
Affected object (AO)	Daddy eating (AO = pizza)	Jill eating (AO = bagel)
	Pull (AO = chair)	Pull (AO = wagon)
Action		
Actor	Going (A = child)	Go (A = car)
Affected object	Open (AO = car door)	Open (AO = jar)
Situation	Come (downstairs)	Come (out of the house)
Grammatical		
Subject	Pull	I pulling
Object	Pull	Pull me
SVO	Drop	My drop my cup
Locative	Go	Go there
Preposition	My fall	My fall down
Negation	I bite	No bite
Morphology	Pull	I pulling
Lexical subject	Doggie eating	Daddy eating
Lexical object	Pull me	I pull that

vice versa, for a given verb. An addressee change was coded when a child first made a change in addressee with a given verb.

Semantic Flexibility

Three types of semantic change were coded. An actor change was coded when a child first made a change in actor during the 10 instances of a given verb. For example, the change from the dog to the father as actor in Table 4 instantiated this child's first actor change with *eat*. An affected object change was noted for the instance with each verb when a child used a different affected object from the first instance. For example, the change from the pizza to the bagel as affected object in Table 4 instantiated this child's first affected object change with *eat*. An action change was coded when a child first referred to an action physically different from his or her initial action referent for that verb, according to the ratings described earlier.

Grammatical Flexibility

Nine types of changes were coded as instances of grammatical changes; all consisted of the addition or subtraction of words or morphemes to/from a previously attested frame. Table 4 shows the nine forms followed by examples. The first six forms (subject, object, SVO, locative, preposition, negation) collectively formed the category of syntactic flexibility. Morphological flexibility included any instance in which the child made a change in verb morphology. Past tense uses were vanishingly rare; therefore, we did not have to distinguish irregular past tense forms from regularized past tense forms (e.g., "fell" vs. "falled"). In addition to the foregoing measures of flexibility of syntactic frames in which the target verbs were used, measures of the flexibility of verb use with respect to the lexical items filling the subject and object roles were coded. Lexical subject and lexical object changes included any instance in which the child made a change in the lexical term used in the subject or object position. For example, a change from saying "I pull" to "Baby pull" was coded as a change in lexical subject use. In contrast, a change from "pull" to "I pull" constituted a change in syntax.

In sum, a total of 14 kinds of flexibility were coded for in the children's first uses of their first verbs. The measures of pragmatic flexibility were designed to address the relatively narrow question of the degree to which the children's verb uses were context bound: Children who use their verbs only as commands, and/or only in addressing their mother (when other addressees were available), may only understand these verbs as tied to a specific context of use. The measures of semantic flexibility were designed to address the core questions of extendability: to what extent were the children able to use their verbs with a variety of actors and affected objects, and to refer (appropriately) to different actions? Children who use each of their verbs with only a single actor or affected object, referring to only one instantiation of that verb, may not have acquired a principle of extendability that applies to verb meanings. The measures of grammatical flexibility were designed to address the core questions of productivity: To what extent were the children able to use their verbs in different (appropriate) sentence frames and/or with different morphology? Children who use each of their verbs in only a single frame may not yet have abstract frames that are represented or that operate independently of their verbs. The semantic and grammatical flexibility measures were also used to address the question of whether children use light verbs as pathbreakers to an adult/abstract grammar: Are light verbs used with greater semantic or grammatical flexibility than heavy verbs? These latter measures were also the relevant ones for the analyses concerning how semantic and grammatical flexibility of verb use might be related during language development.

The coding was first performed by the third author and then checked in its entirety by the first author. Disagreements were resolved by discussion.

For each verb for a given child, the following were calculated for each type of flexibility: (a) which of the first 10 uses manifested the change in usage, (b) how many days elapsed between first use and first different use, and (c) how many different uses for each category occurred within the 10 instances. Variability in how children use their first verbs can arise both from differences among children and from differences among verbs. In order to investigate both sources of variability, all analyses were conducted: (1) treating children as the random factor and calculating measures for each child by averaging across the verbs they produced and (2) treating verbs as the random factor and calculating measures for each verb averaging across the children who produced them (H. Clark, 1973). Means and statistical analyses are reported for both types of calculations.

III. A GENERAL DESCRIPTION OF EARLY VERB GROWTH AND USE

In this chapter, we describe the emergence and early growth of verb use in the eight typically developing, English-learning children who were the participants in this diary study. On average, the children produced the first instance of one of the target verbs by 18 months of age and added verbs (from the list of target verbs) to their productive lexicons at a rate of 3.21 verbs per month. On average, just over 1 month elapsed from the 1st to the 10th instance of use. Table 5 presents the data for each child, listing age at first use of the first verb, mean age of first use of all verbs, number of target verbs produced over the course of the study (i.e., between 3 and 13 months; see Table 3), and mean days to reach 10 instances.

As Table 5 shows, the children varied considerably both in age of onset of verb use and in number of days to reach 10 instances of use. Some children (e.g., Carl) took very little time (e.g., on average, under 4 days) to produce 10 instances once use of a verb began; other children (e.g., Sam) took more time (e.g., on average, over 2 months). For four children, all 10 instances were produced on the same day for at least one verb; for the other four children, the shortest number of days to reach 10 instances ranged from 2 to 18 days (Ned = 2, Carrie = 5, Stacey = 7, Sam = 18). Figure 1 presents the children's cumulative target verb vocabulary over the course of the study. The children can be grouped into early verb learners (Sam, Ned, Carrie, Heather, and Stacey) and later verb learners (Elaine, Carl, Mae). Most of the early verb learners (except for Sam) were also fast learners, with steep increases in target verb vocabulary over time. Most of the late verb learners (except for Elaine) were also slower learners, with more gradual increases in target verb vocabulary. The correlation between the age at which children produced their first of the target verbs and the average age at which they first produced all the target verbs used during this study was significant, $r(n = 8) = .81$, $p < .001$.

Table 6 presents the analogous data by verb, also revealing much variability. The average age of onset across all verbs was 649.96 days

TABLE 5

OVERALL VERB DEVELOPMENT, BY CHILD

Child	Number of Verbs	Age First Verb Produced (Days)	Mean Age of Onset Across Verbs	Mean Number of Days to Reach 10 Instances
Carl	24	603	759.17	3.17
Carrie	30	564	744.93	20.03
Elaine	19	602	674.89	24.95
Heather	31	584	632.97	49.55
Mae	31	577	744.93	35.60
Ned	14	511	532.85	22.64
Sam	31	546	600.10	67.48
Stacey	20	491	534.94	58.39
Mean	24.63	559.75	653.10	35.23
SD	6.48	41.15	92.76	21.73

($SD = 38.47$); *open* was on average the earliest produced whereas *give* was on average the latest of these 34 verbs to be produced. On average, verbs reached the 10-instance mark 37.39 days after their first use ($SD = 16.71$); *clap* took the fewest days to reach 10 instances and *wave* took the most, although the data on *clap* and *wave* are the least reliable, being used by only two children. Two verbs were produced by all 8 children (*want, wash*); on average, each verb was produced by 5.79 children ($SD = 1.59$).

Across verbs, the number of children who produced the verb within the window of this study correlated negatively with the average age at which

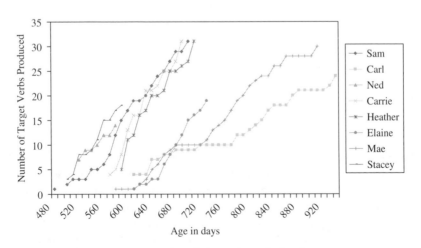

FIGURE 1.—Cumulative verb vocabulary by age.

TABLE 6

OVERALL VERB DEVELOPMENT, BY VERB

Verb	Number of Children	Mean Age of Onset Across Children	Rank Order of Acquisition	Mean Number of Days to Reach 10 Instances
Bite	7	592.71	3	44.29
Bring	3	704.67	32	47.33
Clap	2	668.50	24	11.50
Come	8	616.50	10	26.38
Cry	7	680.57	27	65.86
Cut	7	645.57	17	34.00
Drop	5	645.20	16	57.20
Eat	7	604.71	5	47.14
Fall	5	614.20	8	55.60
Give	5	741.60	34	40.60
Go	7	589.86	2	26.00
Hold	6	663.67	23	23.00
Jump	7	643.14	15	61.00
Kiss	6	661.33	19	50.50
Lay	4	599.25	4	27.00
Like	6	710.83	33	33.00
Look	7	626.29	12	17.57
Move	3	696.00	30	35.67
Need	6	638.33	14	27.67
Open	7	587.57	1	17.29
Pull	5	671.20	25	77.60
Push	6	608.17	6	14.83
Put	5	663.00	22	48.40
Roll	6	680.50	28	30.67
Run	7	672.71	26	38.29
See	6	612.17	7	29.57
Sit	7	616.57	11	13.83
Stop	5	700.00	31	25.60
Take	5	661.80	20	38.80
Throw	5	614.20	9	35.60
Walk	7	637.43	13	23.71
Want	8	651.13	18	43.75
Wash	8	662.13	21	29.88
Wave	2	687.00	29	72.00

that verb first appeared in the speech of the children who produced it, $r(n = 34) = -.39$, $p < .05$. Thus, verbs that were produced early were the verbs that were produced by more children within the span of the study. Also, the 21 verbs that were produced by at least six of the children (*bite, come, cry, cut, eat, go, hold, jump, kiss, like, look, need, open, push, run, roll, sit, see, walk, want, wash*) reached 10 instances of use in an average of 33.24 days ($SD = 14.42$ days), whereas the 13 verbs produced by fewer than six of the children (*bring, clap, drop, fall, give, lay, move, pull, put, stop, take, throw, wave*) reached 10 instances of use in an average of 44.07 days ($SD = 18.52$), a statistically reliable difference, $t(32) = 1.91$, $p < .05$, one-tailed, Cohen's $d = 0.67$. In sum, those verbs that were the most widely acquired were also the earliest acquired.

The mean age of first use for light ($M = 645.43$ days, $SD = 96.40$) and heavy verbs ($M = 635.13$ days, $SD = 83.19$) did not differ, nor did these verb subclasses differ in mean number of days to reach 10 instances (M [light] $= 31.82$, $SD = 18.08$; M [heavy] $= 36.30$, $SD = 23.74$). Similarly, transitive (T), intransitive (I), and alternating (A) verbs did not differ in their mean ages of first use (M [T] $= 663.85$, $SD = 114.53$, M [I] $= 629.61$, $SD = 90.87$, M [A] $= 626.89$, $SD = 81.33$) nor in their mean number of days to reach 10 instances (M [T] $= 32.28$, $SD = 20.39$, M [I] $= 31.9$, $SD = 24.17$, M [A] $= 37.19$, $SD = 24.37$). Thus, the data indicate that the variability on these measures of the timing of emergence and the rate of early use was not systematically related to either the heavy–light distinction among verbs or to the transitive, intransitive, and alternating distinction among verbs.

All children produced at least one grammatical subject with at least one verb, but only 32% ($SD = 22\%$) of the verb tokens were produced with overt subjects. Overt direct objects were more common, produced with an average of 46% of the tokens ($SD = 25\%$). Each child produced at least two tokens of subject–verb–object (SVO) frames, with 24% ($SD = 19\%$) of transitive or alternating verb tokens in SVO frames. Similar findings were obtained when calculations were performed by verb: 35% of verb tokens were produced with overt subjects ($SD = 20\%$), 45% of transitive or alternating verb tokens were produced with overt objects ($SD = 30\%$), and 24% of transitive/alternating verb tokens were produced in SVO frames ($SD = 21\%$). On average, then, the children more frequently produced verbs with direct objects than with subjects, $t(7) = 1.85$, $p = .052$, one-tailed, $d = 0.59$, and transitive and alternating verbs appeared with direct objects more frequently than they appeared with subjects, $t(24) = 2.36$, $p = .013$ one-tailed, $d = 0.39$. Six of the eight children, and 18 of the 25 relevant verbs, followed this pattern. As expected, uses of verb inflections and prepositions were much less frequent, with inflections included with 6% of children's verb tokens ($SD = 9\%$; when calculated by verb, $M = 7\%$ and $SD = 11\%$) and prepositions included with 11% of their verb tokens ($SD = 5\%$; when calculated by verb, $M = 24\%$, $SD = 25\%$).

As did the age of onset and rate of production measures for these verbs, the measures of grammatical use revealed wide variation among the children and among the verbs. The percent of verb tokens produced with subjects varied from 74% (Carrie) to 1% (Ned), the percent of transitive or alternating verb tokens produced with direct objects varied from 77% (Stacey) to 17% (Sam), and the percent of transitive or alternating verb tokens produced in SVO frames ranged from 59% (Carrie) to 2% (Ned). Verbs also varied in the percent of tokens produced with subjects, from 70% (*wave*) to 0% (*look*, *stop*), transitive and alternating verbs varied in the percent of tokens produced with direct objects, from 94% (*want*) to 0% (*jump*, *lay*), and the percent of tokens appearing in SVO frames ranged from 73% (*want*) to 0% (five verbs: *jump*, *lay*, *stop*, *push*, *open*). Variation in morphological and preposition use was also observed: Only five of the children produced any verb tokens with the "-ing" suffix and the percent of such tokens ranged from 23% (Carrie) to 1% (Ned). Fifteen of the 34 verbs appeared with "-ing," and the percent of such tokens ranged from 0% (9 verbs) to 37% (*cry*). Other verbal morphology included 4 uses of third person singular "-s" (two children contributing) and 10 uses of the past tense (three children contributing). Six of the children produced verb tokens with prepositions and the percent of such tokens ranged from 17.7% (Sam) to 4.6% (Carrie). Prepositions were produced with 15 of the 34 verbs, and the percent of such tokens ranged from 90% (*lay*) to 1% (*look*). Thus, the children's first verb-containing utterances were frequently not full SVO structures and typically lacked morphological inflection, consistent with the utterance length limitations characteristic of this age and with the telegraphic nature of early word combinations. There was also a trend in the data such that the children who were older when they began using these verbs used them more frequently in full SVO frames than did the earlier verb users, $r(n = 8) = .63$, $p = .09$.

Table 7 displays the percent of tokens including subjects, objects, prepositions, "-ing," SVO frames, and verb-only utterances used with light and heavy verbs. In contrast to the null findings with respect to the timing of emergence and rate of production measures, these measures of grammatical frame use revealed several differences between these two categories of verb. Light verbs appeared significantly more frequently in SVO frames than did heavy verbs, and light verbs were significantly less likely to appear in verb-only utterances. However, both verb subclasses included verbs with few verb-only uses (fewer than 30% of tokens [light verbs in boldface]: **bring**, clap, cry, fall, **give**, hold, lay, like, need, **put**, **take**, **want**, wave), many verb-only uses (>60% of tokens: bite, **go**, move, pull, push, see, stop, throw, walk), and intermediate verb-only uses (between 30% and 59% of tokens: **come**, cut, eat, jump, kiss, look, pull, roll, run, sit, wash). Trends in the analyses both by children and by verbs suggest that "-ing" appeared more frequently with heavy than with light verbs.

Table 8 displays for the transitive, intransitive, and alternating verbs the percent of tokens used with subjects, objects, prepositions, "-ing," and SVO frames. Children used transitive verbs with both objects and SVO frames more frequently than alternating verbs. Moreover, the by-verbs analysis revealed significant effects of verb type for both the percent of tokens with subjects and

TABLE 7

GRAMMATICAL PROPERTIES OF LIGHT AND HEAVY VERB USE

Grammatical Item (Proportions)	Light		Heavy					
	Means	SD	Means	SD	t	df*	p	Cohen's d
I. By children								
Tokens with subjects	.33	.22	.34	.21	− 0.36	7	ns	
Tokens with objects	.75	.23	.38	.24	5.31	7	.001	1.57
Tokens with SVO	.42	.30	.19	.16	2.88	7	.02	0.96
Tokens with "-ing"	.03	.05	.08	.11	− 1.46	7	ns	
Tokens with P	.09	.10	.07	.07	1.09	7	ns	
Tokens verb-only	.25	.21	.40	.21	5.14	7	.001	0.71
II. By verbs								
Tokens with subjects	.37	.24	.34	.19	0.37	32	ns	
Tokens with objects	.73	.17	.38	.28	2.64	23	.01	1.32
Tokens with SVO	.43	.23	.23	.26	1.52	23	ns	
Tokens with "-ing"	.04	.08	.08	.12	− 1.86	32	ns	
Tokens with P	.12	.19	.10	.21	0.17	32	ns	
Tokens verb-only	.24	.24	.42	.26	1.76	32	.087	0.70

Note.—*The df decrease for the % tokens with objects and with SVO (subject–verb–object) by items because only the transitive and alternating verbs are included.

the percent of tokens with "-ing": Transitive verbs appeared with subjects more frequently than alternating verbs, and intransitive verbs appeared with "-ing" more frequently than either transitive or alternating verbs.

In sum, this group of typically developing middle socioeconomic status children began to use verbs in their spontaneous speech at an average age of 18 months (560 days). Within the following 3–11 months, the children produced an average of 25 of the targeted 34 common verbs in at least 10 utterances. The nature of these children's first uses of their first verbs supports some generalizations about early verb development. Contrary to the picture of idiosyncratic development suggested by studies that only sampled children's speech (see chapter I), these diary data indicate that some verbs are consistently acquired earlier than others, and these early-appearing verbs are also used by more children. (We can reject sampling probability as the cause of a spurious relation between these two variables because of the unique nature of this data set—mothers recorded all verb uses.) Children who produced their first verb earlier tended to be faster learners overall. The children produced at least some of their first uses of first verbs in multiword utterances, but they varied widely in the percent of verb uses that were in word combinations. Consistently, though, verbs were more likely to be combined with direct objects than with subjects and combinations with prepositions and morphology use were rare.

TABLE 8

GRAMMATICAL PROPERTIES OF TRANSITIVE, INTRANSITIVE, AND ALTERNATING VERB USE

Grammatical Item (Proportions)	Transitive		Intransitive		Alternating		F/t	df*	p	Cohen's d
	Means	SD	Means	SD	Means	SD				
I. By children										
Tokens with subjects	.40	.24	.30	.22	.27	.21	.78	2.21	ns	
Tokens with objects	.64	.31			.27	.20	5.33	7	.001	1.42
Tokens with SVO	.35	.28			.12	.11	3.70	7	.007	1.08
Tokens with "-ing"	.01	.01	.11	.14	.06	.10	2.24	2.21	ns	
Tokens with P					Negligible for all verb types					
II. By verbs										
Tokens with subjects	.49	.18	.36	.20	.26	.17	4.50	2.31	.01**	
Tokens with objects	.72	.20			.27	.21	5.13	22	.001	2.18
Tokens with SVO	.51	.25			.13	.14	4.94	22	.001	2.03
Tokens with "-ing"	.01	.03	.16	.15	.05	.08	5.99	2.31	.006**	
Tokens with P	.09	.19	.13	.18	.10	.23	0.23	2.31	ns	

Note. —*The *df* decrease for the % tokens with objects and with SVO (subject–verb–object) by items because only the transitive and alternating verbs are included.
**For % tokens with subjects, transitive versus alternating post hoc comparison yields a significant difference, $t(22) = 3.13$, $p = .004$, $d = 1.32$. For % tokens with "-ing," the intransitive versus transitive post hoc comparison yielded a significant difference, $t(17) = -2.83$, $p = .01$, $d = 1.35$, as did the intransitive versus alternating comparison, $t(23) = 2.43$, $p = .02$, $d = .98$.

This pattern of combinatorial verb use differed somewhat by verb subclass. Light verbs were produced with more objects and more frequently in SVO frames, and heavy verbs were produced with more "-ing" forms. However, contrary to the hypothesis that light verbs would serve as "pathbreakers" to grammatical structures, we found no evidence that light verbs were produced earlier in children's speech than heavy verbs. Of the 11 verbs produced before the age of 620 days (on average), some were light (*come, go*), but others were not (*throw, sit, see, push, open, lay, fall, eat, bite*). And light verbs did appear less frequently in verb-only utterances, supporting Snedeker and Gleitman's (2004) suggestion that light verbs are the products rather than the engines of grammatical acquisition. Further analyses of this hypothesis will be considered in chapters V and VI, when we discuss the grammatical flexibility of light and heavy verbs as a group and individually. Finally, transitive verbs appeared with subjects, objects, and SVO frames more frequently than alternating verbs did, while intransitive verbs appeared with "-ing" forms more frequently than either transitive or alternating verbs. We further investigate these patterns of differences among children and among verbs in chapter VI.

Having painted this general picture of verb emergence and growth in these eight children's use of their first verbs, we turn now to a more detailed description of the communicative functions these verbs served and the meanings that they expressed.

IV. PRAGMATIC AND SEMANTIC FLEXIBILITY IN EARLY VERB USE

In this chapter, we present analyses that address the questions of how extendable first verb uses are in terms of function and meaning. The model of the child as a conservative language learner suggests that children should restrict the functions of their first verbs to those they have heard in input and thus, to the degree that input illustrates only some functions children's verb uses, should show a restricted range of functions for each verb when it is first used (Golinkoff et al., 1995; Maguire et al., 2006; Tomasello, 1992). The conservative-child model also suggests that children should initially use some verbs with reference to only the event that verb was first paired with. The evidence that verb use in maternal speech to children is frequently tied to particular settings (Naigles & Hoff, 2006) suggests that a conservative language learner would be similarly restrictive in verb production. Such a conservative child might, for example, use "throw" only as a command to throw a ball or "eat" only in reference to eating cookies but not pizza, or only in reference to themselves eating but not their parents. If children's initial uses of their early verbs are underextended in the same fashion as early noun uses, we should expect to find the diary records of the children's initial verb instances replete with identical entries down the 10 rows. In contrast, if verb meanings and functions are extended almost from the beginning, then we should expect to find the diary records containing a varied set of entries even within the first 10 uses of children's very early verbs.

To test these predictions, we describe the pragmatic, semantic, and action flexibility that the children demonstrated in their first 10 uses of the target verbs they produced during the course of this study, and we compare the measures of flexibility for light and heavy verbs, and for transitive, intransitive, and alternating verbs.

PRAGMATIC FLEXIBILITY

Commands and Descriptions

The pragmatic categories of "command" and "description" together account for 98.6 % of the verb-containing utterances in the diary records; 45.4% of verb uses were in commands and 53.2% were in descriptions. These proportions are in line with other findings for this age group (e.g., Vasilyeva, Waterfall, & Huttenlocher, 2008). All of the children used at least one verb in both sorts of utterances. On average, the children produced both commands and descriptions with 53% of their verbs (*SD* = 13%); the range was from 33% (Stacey) to 71% (Carl). They produced commands only with an average of 21% of their verbs (*SD* = 16%) and descriptions only with an average of 25% of their verbs (*SD* = 14%). Four children used more verbs only in commands than only in descriptions, three children used more verbs only in descriptions than only with commands, and one child used the same number of verbs only with commands and only in descriptions (see Figure 2). Thus, different children tended to use language for different communicative functions; however, all children were able to use at least some of their verbs in utterances serving different functions.

Some verbs were more likely to be used in commands and others in descriptions; the average percent of children using a verb in both utterance types within their first 10 instances was 53% (*SD* = 27). Some verbs were used in both utterance types by all of the children (*bring, take*), whereas

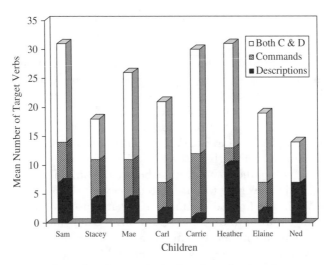

FIGURE 2.—Communicative functions of early verb uses.

others never were (*fall* and *drop* were used only in descriptions). Seven verbs (*bite, bring, kiss, pull, push, take,* and *walk*) were used both as commands and descriptions by 80% of the children or more, *stop* was used only in commands by 80% of the children, and *like* was used only in descriptions by 80% of the children. These findings seem to follow from the meanings and typical usages of these verbs: *Fall* and *drop* were used most commonly in reference to the actions of inanimate objects, which are not likely to respond well to commands; moreover, as *like* is a verb of internal volition, it is not likely to be the subject of commands (children do not tell adults to like things). Thus, where verbs were tied to specific functions the restricted use seems explicable in terms of the verb's meaning rather reflecting context bound representation on the part of the child. The majority of verbs were used as both commands and descriptions by the majority of children, and when verbs were used to serve both functions, the second function appeared on average by the fourth instance of use of that verb ($M = 4.32$, $SD = 0.89$) and within 16.91 days ($SD = 11.83$).

Some differences emerged between light and heavy verbs in terms of these pragmatic properties. The children were more likely to use light verbs only as commands than heavy verbs, $Ms = 0.39$ (0.30) and 0.14 (0.12), respectively, $t(7) = 3.01$, $p = .05$, Cohen's $d = 1.09$, and less likely to use light verbs only as descriptions, M (light) = 0.08 (0.13), M (heavy) = 0.30 (0.17), $t(7) = -3.00$, $p = .05$, Cohen's $d = 1.92$. Similarly, light verbs tended to be used more frequently than heavy verbs only as commands, $Ms = 0.33$ (0.27) and 0.16 (0.25), respectively, $t(32) = 1.66$, $p = .10$, Cohen's $d = 0.67$, and less frequently only as descriptions, M (light) = 0.10 (0.09), M (heavy) = 0.32 (0.31), $t(32) = -1.92$, $p = .10$, Cohen's $d = 0.79$.

Addressee Flexibility (For Command Utterances Only)

When using verbs to command, all children used at least one verb with more than one addressee; however, again, there was considerable variability among children in the addressee flexibility they demonstrated. Figures 3a and 3b show the mean percent of verbs with which the children used more than one addressee and the mean instance at which the first change in addressee took place. On average, the children displayed addressee flexibility with 50% of their verbs ($SD = 21\%$). For those verbs that were used flexibly, the children did so on average before the fifth instance ($M = 4.72$, $SD = 0.58$), and on average within 13.29 days ($SD = 10.03$ days) of the first instance. Within the first 10 instances of a verb's use, the number of addressees ranged from 1 to 4 ($M = 1.86$, $SD = 0.66$). Most of the verbs (81.25%) were used with more than one addressee from at least one child; however, six verbs (*wave, like, jump, cry, clap,* and *bring*) were used with only one addressee by each child. Verbs on average were used with addressee

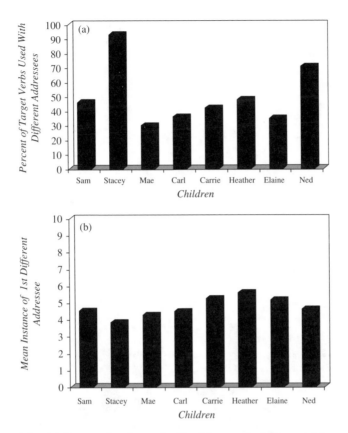

FIGURE 3.—(a) Percent of verbs used with addressee flexibility and (b) onset of addressee flexibility in early verb use.

flexibility by 41% of the children ($SD = 26\%$). Verbs in commands were used with a different addressee from the first instance within, on average, 14.47 days of the first use ($SD = 19.96$ days) and by the fifth instance of the use of that verb ($M = 4.36$, $SD = 1.25$). When the measures of addressee flexibility are compared for the light and heavy subclasses, none of the analyses by child yielded significant differences. The analyses by verb yielded one difference: Light verbs were used with significantly more addressees than heavy verbs, M (light) = 2.04 (.55), M (heavy) = 1.58 (.44), $t(30) = 2.36$, $p = .05$, Cohen's $d = 0.98$.

In sum, when verbs first enter children's productive lexicons, children do not seem to uniformly restrict these verbs to a single utterance function, nor to a single addressee. They use about half of their verbs in both commands and descriptions, and they direct their commands, with about half of their verbs, to multiple addressees. One limitation of change of addressee as a measure of children's flexibility of verb use is that, over the course of a day, these children have only a limited number of possible addressees: mother, sibling, pet, and father. Thus, children who reach their 10 instances of a given verb quickly might be less likely to demonstrate addressee flexibility because fewer different addressees are available.

SEMANTIC FLEXIBILITY

Action Flexibility

Figures 4a and 4b show for each child the percent of verbs used in reference to more than one action and the mean instance at which the first change in action referent occurred. On average, children made reference to more than one action with 38% of their verbs (*SD* = 19%). For those verbs

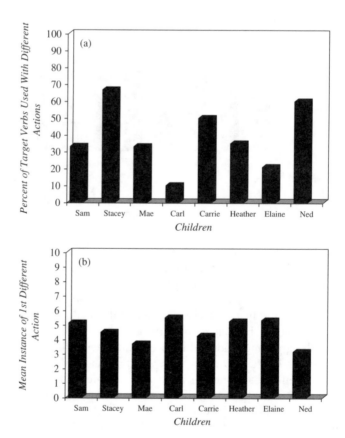

FIGURE 4.—(a) Percent of verbs used with action flexibility and (b) onset of action flexibility in early verb use.

showing action flexibility, children's first new action use occurred on average before the fifth instance ($M = 4.6$, $SD = 0.85$) and within 15.54 days ($SD = 13.50$) after the first instance. The number of actions per verb within the first 10 instances ranged from one to four; six of the eight children referred to at least three different actions with at least one verb. Across verbs, an average of 33% of the children ($SD = 20\%$) referred to more than one action within the first 10 instances of producing a verb. *Come* was used to refer to more than one action by six of the children; *put* and *open* were used to refer to more than one action by five of the children. The first change in action reference occurred on average by the fifth instance ($M = 5.1$, $SD = 1.99$) and on average within 27.14 days of the first use ($SD = 35.77$).

Actor Flexibility

Figures 5a and 5b show for each child the percent of verbs used in reference to more than one actor and the mean instance at which the first change in actor occurred. All children used at least 50% of their verbs in

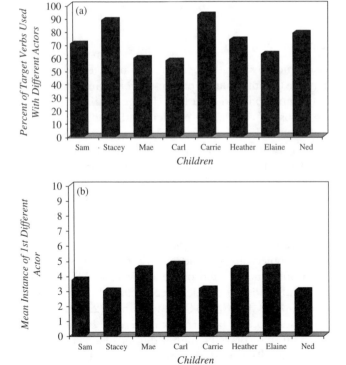

FIGURE 5.—(a) Percent of verbs used with actor flexibility and (b) onset of actor flexibility in early verb use.

reference to more one actor. On average, children made reference to more than one actor with 73% of their verbs ($SD = 13\%$). For those verbs showing actor flexibility, the first new actor use occurred on average before the fourth instance ($M = 3.9$, $SD = 0.77$) and within 15.79 days ($SD = 12.06$) after the first instance. The number of actors per verb within the first 10 instances ranged from 1 to 5 ($M = 2.68$, $SD = 1.0$). Across verbs, an average of 76% of the children ($SD = 20\%$) referred to more than one actor within the first 10 instances of producing a verb; eight of the verbs were used with different actors by all the children. The first change in actor reference occurred on average before the fourth instance ($M = 3.85$, $SD = 1.01$) and on average within 16.91 days of the first use ($SD = 13.91$).

The percent of children's verb uses that referred to themselves as actors ranged from 11% (Stacey) to 70% (Carl). On average, 51% ($SD = 18.1\%$) of children's first 10 uses of these early verbs concerned themselves as actors. Among verbs, the percent of uses that referred to self as actors ranged from 0% for the verbs *cry*, *look*, *move*, *open*, and *pull* (the latter four primarily in commands) to 100% for the verbs *clap*, *like*, and *want*. *Cry* was used exclusively in reference to infant siblings or fictional characters. Mean percent of self as actor uses calculated across verbs was 50.8% ($SD = 30\%$).

Affected Object Flexibility

Figures 6a and 6b show the percent of transitive and alternating verbs used in reference to more than one affected object and the mean instance at which the children produced their first change in affected object reference. (Intransitive verbs, of course, do not have affected objects.) Children referred to different affected objects on average with 89% of their verbs ($SD = 9.8\%$). For those verbs that were used flexibly, the children referred to a new affected object on average before the fourth instance ($M = 3.33$, $SD = 0.79$) and within 11.68 days ($SD = 7.93$) of the first instance. The number of affected objects referred to within the first 10 instances ranged from 1 to 8 ($M = 4.69$, $SD = 1.77$). The proportion of children who made reference to more than one affected object averaged 79% across verbs ($SD = 31$). Twelve of the transitive and alternating verbs were used with different affected objects by all children, whereas only two verbs (*jump*, *lay*) appeared with only one affected object in every child's productions. The first change in affected object reference occurred on average before the fourth instance ($M = 3.34$, $SD = 0.97$) and within 12.40 days ($SD = 7.61$).

The above descriptions (and compare Figures 5a, 5b and 6a, 6b) suggest that the children displayed a higher degree of affected object flexibility than actor flexibility. Paired t tests confirmed this difference for two of the three flexibility measures: By children, the t tests revealed a significant difference in the percent of verbs showing actor compared with affected

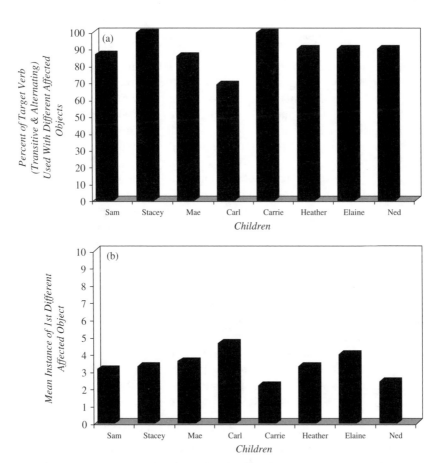

FIGURE 6.—(a) Percent of verbs used with affected object flexibility and (b) onset of affected object flexibility in early verb use.

object flexibility, $t(7) = 6.02$, $p = .0005$, Cohen's $d = 1.39$, and a significant difference in when the first different actor was produced compared with when the first different affected object was produced, $t(7) = 3.42$, $p = .01$, $d = 0.73$. Comparison of the number of days to actor and affected object change showed a trend in the same direction, $t(7) = 1.599$, $p < .10$, $d = 0.40$. By verbs (only the transitive and alternating verbs are included), the t tests revealed significant differences for the mean instance of change measure, $t(22) = 2.16$, $p = .04$, $d = 0.62$, and the number of days to first change measure, $t(22) = 2.78$, $p = .01$, $d = 0.37$, but not for the percent of children showing flexibility, $t(24) < 1$, ns. (The degrees of freedom differ in these analyses because two verbs displayed no affected object flexibility.)

We next compared the different verb subclasses in terms of actor and affected object flexibility. Children produced a significantly higher percent of their light verbs with reference to different affected objects than that they did for heavy verbs, M (light) = 0.98, SD = 0.06, M (heavy) = 0.81, SD = 0.20, $t(7)$ = 2.29, p = .055, Cohen's d = 1.15, and light verbs tended to be produced with different actors by a higher percent of children than did heavy verbs, M (light) = 0.87, SD = 0.18, M (heavy) = 0.72, SD = 0.19, $t(32)$ = 1.88, p = .068, Cohen's d = 0.80. There were no differences among the categories of transitive, intransitive, and alternating verbs in actor flexibility and no difference between transitive and alternating verbs in affected object flexibility.

These data reveal a picture of pragmatic and semantic flexibility in early verb use. For example, these children were very likely to use *eat* in reference to multiple foods and multiple eaters. Eating, for them, was not a restricted category that applied to a single type of situation but one that applied across (at least) different foods being eaten (which are, of course, eaten in different ways—cookies are chewed, ice cream is licked, cereal is slurped) and different people and animals doing the eating (showing that the children were able to generalize across different mouth motions to an inclusive rather than restricted meaning for *eat*). This picture suggests that children's first verb uses differ from their first noun uses, which can be quite inflexible (Dromi, 1987; Harris et al., 1988).

The present findings also differ from other descriptions of early verb use in the literature. Contrary to the predictions of Huttenlocher et al. (1983), children's very first verb uses were not consistently in reference to their own actions or relations; children were just as likely to talk about someone else's actions as their own. Interestingly, more flexibility was observed with affected objects than with actors; we conjecture that this is because there is a greater range of possible affected objects in a child's home (e.g., toys, food, household items) than of possible actors (e.g., animates). Light verbs were produced with more varied affected objects than heavy verbs, which is consistent with the notion that light verbs apply to a wider range of items (one can *bring* just about anything) than heavy verbs (usually, one *eats* only food, *kisses* only animates, and *rolls* only round things; see also Goodman & Sethuraman, 2006; Snedeker & Gleitman, 2004; Valian et al., 2006). Overall, then, these analyses of the functions and semantics of early verb use suggest that when verbs enter children's productive lexicons they are not tied to particular uses but are available to serve multiple communicative functions, to refer to a variety of actions, and to refer to the actions and relations they denote with multiple agents and affected objects.

V. PRODUCTIVITY AND GRAMMATICAL FLEXIBILITY IN EARLY VERB USE

In this chapter, we present analyses that address the question of how grammatically productive and flexible children are in their initial uses of early-acquired verbs. The conservative-child model predicts that children will use their verbs only in the morphosyntactic structures they have heard used with that verb. Each verb might have its own range of structures, but that range would be narrower than the full possible range allowed by the adult grammar. If, in contrast, children represent their first verbs as items in an abstract category, with all the morphosyntactic privileges of occurrence allowed by the adult grammar, then in early verb use, each verb should be used in a wider range of structures—and each structure should be used with a wider range of verbs. Thus, the rapid-generalizer model predicts early flexible and productive verb use, whereas the conservative-child model predicts that flexibility and productivity should be achieved only after months or years of input (see Tomasello's [2000] claim that children only become productive with the subject–verb–object [SVO] frame at 3 years of age [pp. 222–223], after they have heard literally thousands of verbs used in SVO in their input).

To index the productivity of children's syntactic frames, we calculated for each child the number of different verbs used each of the following frames: SV, VO, SVO, V+P (preposition or particle), and V-ing. Then, following Ingram (1981, 1989) and Shirai (1998), we tabulated the number of frames that were used with at least three verbs and the number of frames used with at least five different verbs. We also calculated for each frame the percent of all of each child's verb types used in that frame, the age at which the three-verbs-per-frame (3-V) and five-verbs-per-frame (5-V) levels of productivity were reached, and the number of frames that reached 3-V and 5-V productivity when children were 24 and 30 months of age.

To index the grammatical flexibility with which children used their verbs we counted the number of different frames (syntactic flexibility), different inflectional endings (morphological flexibility), different nouns in

49

subject position (lexical subject flexibility) and different nouns in object position (lexical object flexibility) with which each verb appeared in the recorded 10 uses. A frame was coded as different from previously appearing frames if there was an addition or subtraction of a subject, object, locative, preposition, and/or negation term. Morphological differences included the addition or subtraction of a tense/aspect or person marker on the verb. Lexical subject differences involved changes in the lexical item used in the subject position. Lexical object differences involved changes in the lexical item used in the object position. These measures differ from the actor and affected object flexibility measures discussed in the previous chapter because those measures did not require the children to produce the nouns referring to the actors and affected objects, whereas the lexical subject and object measures depend on changes in actual noun use.

GRAMMATICAL PRODUCTIVITY IN FIRST VERB USES

Table 9 displays the mean percent of verb types produced in each frame across children. The children produced SV and VO frames with >60% of all the target verbs they used, and the SVO frame with just under half (40%) of the verbs they used. Thus, these are not frames used with just 1 or 2 verbs. In contrast, they produced the V+P and V-ing frames with <20% of the target verbs they used; as described in chapter III, these frames were used less frequently overall. The children varied in the degree of grammatical productivity they displayed. Heather and Carrie were consistently the most productive children across frames; the child who was least

TABLE 9

PRODUCTIVITY OF VERB USE MEASURES

	Frame				
	SV	VO	SVO	VP	V-ing
Mean % of V types (SD)	61 (28)	62 (29)	41 (26)	18 (15)	15 (14)
Highest % of V types	93.5	100	71.4	35	35
Highest child (# Vs)	Carrie (29)	Heather (21)	Carrie (15)	Sam (11)	Heather (11)
Lowest % of V types	14.3	29.4	4	0	0
Lowest child (# Vs)	Ned (2)	Carl (5)	Sam (1)	Carl, Elaine	Carl
Mean age of 3-V productivity (n)	21.83 (7)	22.28 (8)	23.64 (6)	22.45 (3)	21.11 (4)
Mean age of 5-V productivity (n)	22.6 (7)	23.1 (7)	22.13 (4)	23.43 (5)	21.35 (2)

productive for a given frame varied across four different children (Carl, Elaine, Ned, Sam). Sam was clearly the most variable child, showing the most productivity with the V+P frame and the least with the SVO frame.

Table 9 also shows the children's mean age when they achieved the 3-V and 5-V levels of productivity for each frame. All of these mean ages are younger than 24 months. The number of children included is fewer than seven or eight for the SVO, V+P, and V-ing frames, indicating that these frames manifested less productivity within the span of the study. The children also varied in the number of productive frames (out of five) achieved at 24 and 30 months (see Table 10). At 24 months, most children had achieved at least 3-V productivity with the SV and VO frames (Ned left the study at 20 months, so we know the least about his progression to productivity). Carrie, Heather, and Stacey achieved 5-V productivity before 24 months with almost all frames, whereas Carl achieved less productivity later, closer to 30 months. Elaine, Mae, and Sam occupy the middle ground, having achieved 3-V productivity with four or five frames by 30 months. Because we do not have records of the children's uses of their early verbs past the first 10 instances, the 30-month scores are very likely to underestimate the number of frames used with multiple verbs.

Researchers have proposed that children's linguistic relations "go productive [when] the pattern can participate in free combination with other lexical items that satisfy its typed variables" (Jackendoff, 2004, pp. 188–189). Such "free combination" usually cannot be unequivocally supported from spontaneous speech data, and we do not claim that we have found it here. However, productivity as operationalized by Ingram (1989) and Shirai (1998) can be addressed with spontaneous speech data, and we have found evidence of productivity defined this way in these children's speech. Well before 36 months of age—and frequently even before 24 months of

TABLE 10

NUMBER OF PRODUCTIVE FRAMES (OUT OF FIVE)

Name	At 24 Months		At 30 Months	
	3-V level	5-V level	3-V level	5-V level
Carl	0	0	1	1
Carrie	5	5	5	5
Elaine	2	1	4	2
Heather	5	5	5	5
Mae	0	0	4	4
Ned	1	0	1	0
Sam	3	3	4	3
Stacey	5	4	5	4

age—the children used a number of syntactic frames with multiple verbs, thus showing that frames are not necessarily restricted to specific lexical items.

GRAMMATICAL FLEXIBILITY IN FIRST VERB USES

All eight children used more than one syntactic frame within the first 10 uses of at least one of their verbs. Figures 7a and 7b display for each child the mean instance, across verbs, of the first new frame and the percent of verbs used with more than one frame. On average, the children used 65.6% of their verbs (SD = 18%) in at least two different frames within their first 10 uses; their mean number of different frames per verb was 2.14 (range = 1–5). Thus, this early period did not seem to be one characterized by frozen

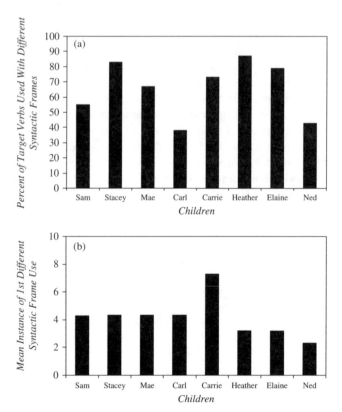

FIGURE 7.—(a) Percent of verbs used with syntactic flexibility and (b) onset of syntactic flexibility in early verb use.

form use. For those verbs that showed flexibility, the first new use occurred on average just after the fourth instance ($M = 4.17$, $SD = 1.47$) and within 15.37 days ($SD = 12.58$) from the first instance. Verbs varied in the percent of children who used them in different frames, from 100% (*fall, give, take, wave*) to 0% (*stop*). On average, verbs were used with different frames by 66% of the children ($SD = 23\%$); the mean number of different frames per verb was 2.20 ($SD = 0.55$). For those children who produced different frames, the first different use occurred on average before the fourth instance ($M = 3.81$, $SD = 1.34$), within 17.77 days ($SD = 16.96$) from the first instance. Most of these instances of syntactic flexibility involved the addition or subtraction of subjects, objects, prepositions, and locatives. Only 12% of frame changes included the use of negation (range 0–36%). On average, 1.8% of utterances included negation.

The addition or subtraction of a preposition was included in our measure of syntactic flexibility; however, this measure captured only whether the preposition slot was filled. It did not capture whether the children used more than one preposition with a given verb and/or a given preposition with more than one verb. Examination of the particular prepositions used showed that of the six children who used prepositions with their verbs, five showed flexibility in their use of prepositions. That is, Ned used only one preposition (*down*) with one verb (*lay*), but Mae, Heather, Carrie, Stacey, and Sam each used at least one verb with multiple prepositions and/or used the same preposition with multiple verbs. For example, Mae used *put* and *pull* each with two prepositions and used *in* and *over* each with two different verbs, and Heather used *put* and *throw* each with two prepositions and *down*, *to*, and *away* each with two different verbs. Sam was by far the most flexible in his preposition use: He used *lay, give, pull, push*, and *put* each with at least two different prepositions and *down* and *in* each with at least two different verbs.

Consistent with descriptions of early combinatorial speech in English learners as telegraphic, these young speakers produced very little inflectional morphology, and, not surprisingly, morphological flexibility was much less pervasive than frame flexibility both across children (appearing in approximately 6% of children's utterances) and across verbs (appearing in approximately 7% of verb uses). Figures 8a and 8b show the percent of verbs with which the children used more than one morphological structure and the instance of the first change; two children produced none of their verbs in more than one morphological form. On average, the children used different morphology with 15.69% of their verbs ($SD = 14.5\%$). For those verbs that showed flexibility, the first different use occurred on average before the fifth instance ($M = 4.55$, $SD = 1.91$) and within 26.98 days ($SD = 21.45$) after the first instance. Verbs were used with different morphological structures by an average of 18% of the children ($SD = 22\%$); the

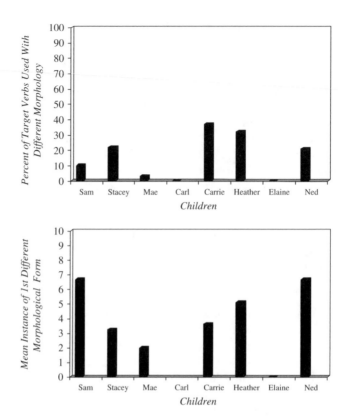

FIGURE 8.—(a) Percent of verbs used with morphological flexibility and (b) onset of morphological flexibility in early verb use.

range extended from 100% of children (*wave*) to 0% of children (14 verbs). The first new use occurred on average before the fifth instance ($M = 4.34$, $SD = 2.29$) and within 22.78 days ($SD = 23.66$). Almost all morphological changes involved the addition of "-ing." A few verbs were produced in the past tense (*drop, wave, give, go, fall*), and one was produced with the third person singular "-s" (*need*). No verbs were produced by any child with more than one overt morphological marker.

Lexical subject flexibility was the norm, with seven of the children (excepting only Ned) using more than one lexical subject with at least one of their verbs. Figures 9a and 9b show for the children the percent of verbs with which they used more than one lexical subject and the instance of the first new lexical subject. On average, the children used more than one different lexical subject with 30.65% of their verbs ($SD = 27.15$). For those verbs that showed flexibility, the first new use appeared on average before the sixth instance ($M = 5.2$, $SD = 1.06$) and within 20.29 days ($SD = 17.79$)

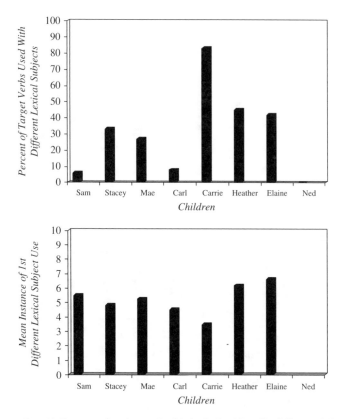

FIGURE 9.—(a) Percent of verbs used with lexical subject flexibility and (b) onset of lexical subject flexibility in early verb use.

after the first lexical subject use. Verbs also varied in the percent of children producing different lexical subjects over the first 10 instances, from 100% (*wave*) to 0 (*throw, stop, push, move, lay*). On average, verbs were used with multiple lexical subjects by 35% of the children ($SD = 26\%$). For those children showing this flexibility, they produced their first new use on average before the fifth instance ($M = 4.77$, $SD = 2.21$) and within 12.74 days ($SD = 16.17$) after their first lexical subject use.

All 8 children used more than one lexical object with at least one transitive or alternating verb. Figures 10a and 10b show for the children the percent of verbs with which they used more than one lexical object and the instance of the first new use. On average, the children used at least two lexical objects with 43.38% of their verbs ($SD = 26.56\%$). For those verbs that showed flexibility, the first different use occurred on average before the fifth instance ($M = 4.13$, $SD = 1.22$) and 20.64 days ($SD = 16.22$) after the first lexical object use. Among the transitive and alternating verbs (the only

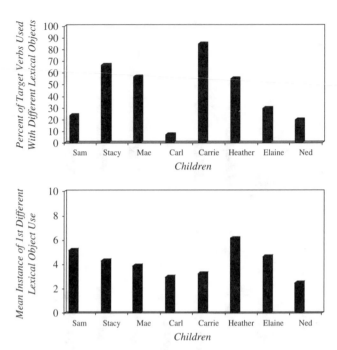

FIGURE 10.—(a) Percent of verbs used with lexical object flexibility and (b) onset of lexical object flexibility in early verb use.

verb categories that take objects) there was considerable variation in the percent of children producing different lexical objects over the first 10 instances, ranging from 100% (*bring*) to 0% (*stop, move*). On average, transitive and alternating verbs appeared with multiple lexical objects in the speech of 46% of the children ($SD = 28\%$). For those children showing this flexibility, the first new use occurred on average before the fifth instance ($M = 4.74$, $SD = 2.06$) and 19.06 days ($SD = 16.09$) after the first lexical object use.

Tables 11 and 12 present means, standard deviations, and statistical comparisons for the measures of grammatical flexibility by verb subclass. Comparison of light and heavy verbs revealed that children produced a significantly higher percent of light verbs than heavy verbs with lexical object flexibility, consistent with the broader meanings of light verbs, and they also produced their first change in lexical object at a significantly earlier instance for light than for heavy verbs. The children tended to produce a higher percent of heavy verbs than light verbs with lexical subject flexibility, although this difference was not statistically significant. Similar findings obtained in the item analyses: Light verbs were produced with different lexical objects by a significantly greater percent of children than

TABLE 11

GRAMMATICAL FLEXIBILITY OF USE FOR LIGHT VERSUS HEAVY VERBS

Grammatical item	Light		Heavy		t	df*	p	Cohen's d
	Mean	SD	Mean	SD				
I. By children								
Proportion Vs with different frames	0.72	0.14	0.69	0.21	0.76	7	ns	
Proportion Vs with different morphology	0.16	0.26	0.20	0.18	−0.3	7	ns	
Proportion Vs with different lexical subjects	0.23	0.26	0.32	0.28	−2.24	7	.06	0.33
Proportion Vs with different lexical objects	0.74	0.36	0.37	0.22	3.38	7	.01	1.24
Mean instance frame change	3.82	1.39	3.54	0.71	0.57	7	ns	
Mean instance morphology change	5.13	3.66	5.73	2.43	Only 3 children contributed			
Mean instance lexical subject change	5.43	3.66	5.10	0.9	Only 5 children contributed			
Mean instance lexical object change	2.98	0.85	4.8	1.47	−9.19	6	.001	1.52
Number of days to frame change	15.93	11.58	14.58	13.08	0.6	7	ns	
Number of days to morphological change	30.50	30.66	26.58	20.18	Only 3 children contributed			
Number of days to lexical subject change	21.34	25.17	16.68	13.04	Only 5 children contributed			
Number of days to lexical object change	18.25	17.18	22.72	16.43	−1.73	6	ns	
II. By verbs								
Proportion Cs with different frames	0.76	0.18	0.67	0.23	1.02	32	ns	
Proportion Cs with different morphology	0.13	0.16	0.20	0.23	−0.8	32	ns	
Proportion Cs with different lexical subjects	0.37	0.19	0.34	0.29	0.23	32	ns	
Proportion Cs with different lexical objects	0.61	0.37	0.32	0.26	2.24	24	.02	1.01
Mean instance frame change	4.08	1.04	3.53	1.23	1.13	32	ns	
Mean instance morphology change	5.62	2.87	4.04	2.13	1.26	19	ns	
Mean instance lexical subject change	4.94	2.83	4.71	2.01	0.24	27	ns	
Mean instance lexical object change	2.95	0.75	5.33	2.02	−2.54	18	.02	1.31
Number of days to frame change	21.35	15.31	15.65	17.6	0.82	32	ns	
Number of days to morphological change	32.25	30.14	20.55	22.40	0.88	19	ns	
Number of days to lexical subject change	17.0	19.37	11.1	14.99	0.87	27	ns	
Number of days to lexical object change	18.67	10.0	19.19	17.96	−0.06	18	ns	

Note.—*df* vary because not all children, nor all verbs, experienced all grammatical changes.

TABLE 12

GRAMMATICAL FLEXIBILITY OF USE FOR TRANSITIVE, INTRANSITIVE, AND ALTERNATING VERBS

Grammatical item	Transitive		Intransitive		Alternating		F/t	df*	p	Cohen's d
	Mean	SD	Mean	SD	Mean	SD				
I. By children										
Proportion Vs with different frames	0.75	0.23	0.78	0.14	0.60	0.30	1.35	2,21	ns	
Proportion Vs with different morphology	0.09	0.09	0.22	0.26	0.19	0.21	0.99	2,21	ns	
Proportion Vs with different lexical subjects	0.23	0.29	0.36	0.29	0.28	0.28	0.38	2,21	ns	
Proportion Vs with different lexical objects	0.56	0.32			0.30	0.27	2.22	7	.06	0.88
Mean instance frame change	5.62	2.0	3.38	0.85	3.2	0.46	2.17	2,21	ns	
Mean instance morphology change	5.0	3.67	5.65	2.5	5.25	2.87	0.05	2,11	ns	
Mean instance lexical subject change	5.62	2.0	4.99	2.35	5.26	1.01	0.87	2,14	ns	
Mean instance lexical object change	3.29	0.8			5.63	1.87	−2.96	6	.025	1.63
Number of days to frame change	16.31	16.14	14.75	12.84	14.65	17.2	0.97	2,21	ns	
Number of days to morphological change	24.68	30.42	36.83	26.15	19.06	13.28	0.6	2,11	ns	
Number of days to lexical subject change	25.17	18.95	17.17	13.24	14.26	13.75	0.66	2,14	ns	
Number of days to lexical object change	15.77	12.62			33.70	36.12	−1.62	6	.12	0.66
II. By verbs										
Proportion Cs with different frames	0.76	0.21	0.77	0.22	0.60	0.19	2.02	2,33	ns	
Proportion Cs with different morphology	0.14	0.15	0.33	0.29	0.10	0.13	4.77	2,33	.01	
Proportion Cs with different lexical subjects	0.33	0.19	0.52	0.29	0.24	0.23	4.33	2,33	.02	
Proportion Cs with different lexical objects	0.61	0.24			0.30	0.26	2.86	22	.01	1.23
Mean instance frame change	4.26	1.18	3.81	1.2	3.14	1.01	3.46	2,31	.04	
Mean instance morphology change	4.3	2.99	4.15	1.62	4.62	2.81	0.07	2,18	ns	
Mean instance lexical subject change	4.52	2.61	4.97	1.94	4.8	2.29	0.09	2,26	ns	
Mean instance lexical object change	3.41	1.31			5.83	1.94	−3.18	18	.005	1.43
Number of days to frame change	21.13	13.93	16.63	19.92	14.75	17.37	0.38	2,31	ns	
Number of days to morphological change	19.4	31.91	22.19	22.49	25.95	22.15	0.11	2,18	ns	
Number of days to lexical subject change	15.28	18.70	15.43	20.66	7.75	5.82	0.71	2,26	ns	
Number of days to lexical object change	14.81	9.69			22.55	19.68	−1.07	18	ns	

Note.—*df* vary because not all children, nor all verbs, experienced all grammatical changes.
% Cs with different morphology: I versus A: $t(23) = -2.7$, $p = .012$, $d = 1.11$.
% Cs with different lexical subjects: I versus A: $t(23) = 2.66$, $p = .013$, $d = 1.10$.
Mean instance frame change: T versus A: $t(22) = 2.67$, $p = .013$, $d = 1.04$.
All other comparisons *ns*.

58

were heavy verbs, and the change in lexical objects was seen at a significantly earlier instance for light than for heavy verbs.

Comparison of children's use of transitive, intransitive, and alternating verbs revealed that children tended to produce different lexical objects with a higher percent of transitive verbs than alternating verbs ($p = .06$); they also produced those different lexical objects at a significantly earlier instance for transitive verbs than for alternating verbs. Analyses by verb yielded a greater number of significant findings: Intransitive verbs appeared with multiple lexical subjects and in multiple morphological contexts in more children's speech than did alternating verbs. Moreover, transitive verbs appeared with lexical object changes for more children than did alternating verbs; transitive verbs also appeared with a different lexical object at a significantly earlier instance. Finally, transitive verbs appeared in new syntactic frames at a significantly earlier instance than did alternating verbs. Overall, then, both transitive and intransitive verbs were associated with more grammatical flexibility than were alternating verbs, and consistent with the arguments each type of verb takes, intransitive verb use was more characterized by flexibility in the subject slot whereas transitive verb use was more characterized by flexibility in the object slot.

To ask whether some types of grammatical flexibility were displayed more than others, two one-way repeated measures ANOVAs (by children and by verbs) were performed, with flexibility as a single factor within-subjects factor with four levels (frame, morphology, lexical subject, and lexical object). The ANOVA by children yielded a significant effect, $F(3, 28) = 7.14$, $p = .001$. Pairwise t tests were performed to discover which categories differed significantly; the Bonferroni correction adjusted the required significance level to .0083 with $\alpha = .05$. Using this correction, only one contrast was significant: Syntactic frame flexibility was significantly greater than morphological flexibility, $t(7) = 7.72$, $p = .0001$, Cohen's $d = 3.04$. The ANOVA by verbs also yielded a significant effect, $F(3, 120) = 23.11$, $p < .0001$. Five contrasts were significant using the same Bonferroni correction: by paired t tests, syntactic flexibility was significantly greater than morphological flexibility and lexical subject flexibility, $ts(33) > 7.25$, $ps < .00001$, Cohen's $ds > 1.25$, and significantly greater than lexical object flexibility, $t(23) = 4.23$, $p = .0003$, $d = 0.78$. Both lexical subject flexibility and lexical object flexibility (by paired t tests) were significantly greater than morphological flexibility, $t(33) = 4.71$, $p = .00004$, $d = 0.71$, and $t(23) = 5.51$, $p < .00001$, $d = 1.11$, respectively.

In sum, the above analyses converge on the conclusion that the eight children in this study all used their first verbs in multiple syntactic environments within the first 10 uses of those verbs. Many verbs were used with different frames—that is, with subjects, with objects, in SVO frames, with prepositions and with negation. Moreover, verbs were used with different subjects and objects, as well, although less frequently than in different frames. That is, across the first instances of verb use, children more frequently changed the frame entirely (via adding or subtracting nouns, Ps, and/or negation) than changed the nouns in the frame. In contrast, much more rarely did the children use their verbs with morphology at all, let alone with morphological changes. Thus, these English-speaking children revealed the flexibility of their early verb use and, by implication, the abstractness of their grammars, more in the syntax of their verb-containing utterances than in the morphology of their verb use. Further research is needed to see whether the same pattern holds in children learning more morphologically rich languages (e.g., Turkish).

The light and heavy verb subclasses did not differ with regard to overall grammatical flexibility; however, light verbs were produced with more and earlier lexical object changes whereas heavy verbs were produced with more and earlier lexical subject changes. Thus, counter to all versions of a "pathbreaking verb" hypothesis (e.g., Chenu & Jisa, 2006; Ninio, 1999), there was no consistent light verb advantage in early grammatical use and flexibility. More detailed comparisons between the light and heavy verbs, addressing the variation among individual children, will be discussed in chapter VI. The transitive/intransitive/alternating verb subclasses also did not differ with regard to overall grammatical flexibility; however, transitive verbs exceeded alternating verbs in their speed of achieving syntactic flexibility and in both amount and speed of achieving lexical object flexibility. Intransitive verbs exceeded alternating verbs in amount of morphological and lexical subject flexibility.

It may seem surprising that the obligatorily transitive and intransitive verbs showed more flexibility than the "permissibly flexible" alternating verbs. This pattern of results may be partially attributable to our definition of flexibility, which included any change in overt realization of grammatical elements and so also included elements such as negation that apply equally across verbs. More important, at this early stage of development the children's output is quite constrained (Valian et al., 2006), and their typically short utterances—especially removed from the context of the conversation—were unrevealing as to whether direct objects were omitted for grammatical (i.e., with alternating verbs) versus processing (i.e., for transitive verbs) reasons. It seems likely that the obligatory nature of direct objects for transitive verbs, then, led to a greater use of objects with those verbs than with alternating verbs, and so resulted in more flexibility. The children's different patterns of use with different subclasses of verbs reflect the target grammar. Two possible explanations also exist for the greater morphological flexibility in children's uses of intransitive compared with alternating verbs. According to a processing demand account, the more minimal (i.e., lacking objects) argument structures of intransitive verbs allows children to devote more of their cognitive resources to selecting subjects and morphological inflections for these verbs. According to a semantic account, the fact that the intransitive verbs in our data set tended to be activity rather than accomplishment verbs explains the difference; the former verbs have already been shown to be used more and earlier with "-ing" (Bloom, Lifter, & Hafitz, 1980; Vendler, 1972; Wagner, 2002). Further research is needed to distinguish between these explanations.

COMPARISON WITH PREVIOUS FINDINGS

Tomasello (1992)

The above findings may seem at odds with Tomasello's (1992, 2000) diary report of his daughter Travis's first verbs and with the Verb Island Hypothesis proposed on the basis of those data. However, these and Tomasello's (1992) productivity findings are actually quite consistent: Both Travis and several of the children in the present study produced the SV, VO, and SVO frames with multiple verbs before the age of 24 months (see Table 8.4 in Tomasello, 1992; 9 verbs were used in the SV frame, 33 verbs were used in the VO frame, and 41 verbs were used in the SVO frame). Tomasello (1992) states, "Travis did indeed begin using word order as a productive syntactic device during the 18–24 month period" (p. 247). The findings that motivated the Verb Island Hypothesis did not have to do with the use of frames with different verbs but with two other findings (see also Tomasello, 2000, p. 213): First, Travis produced no verbs with overlapping privileges of occurrence during the same time period, and second, almost half of her verbs were produced in just one construction type and fewer than one third were produced in two or more. Thus, individual verbs behaved in her speech as "islands" of grammar because their privileges of occurrence were all different and because each one was restricted to being used in only one construction. The verb diary records collected for the present study do not permit addressing the first finding regarding overlap among verbs in their uses (i.e., because we have only 10 instances for each verb), but they do provide data at odds with Tomasello's finding that individual verbs were limited in the range of constructions in which they appear. The children in the present study used their first verbs both with and without subjects, with and without direct objects, with varied prepositions, and so on. In fact, they produced almost 70% of their verbs in more than one syntactic frame by the 10th instance of use. What might account for this discrepancy between our findings and Tomasello's? One possibility is that both Tomasello and the present study accurately characterize the participants in each study, and the participants differ. It could be that flexibility of early verb use varies among

61

children and that Travis represented one extreme of this variability. Another possibility is that the different findings reflect the different ways in which flexibility was coded in the two studies. We consider each of these possibilities in the following analyses. First, we reanalyze the data from our child participants according to Tomasello's method and compare the results with those obtained from Travis. Performing this exercise led us to our second analysis, which involves a more detailed coding of argument use by verb subclass.

One basis for Tomasello's characterization of Travis's grammar as containing verb islands comes from his analysis of the arguments Travis used with her verbs. Tomasello found that Travis was most likely to use her verbs either in single-word utterances or with only a single argument. Importantly for the claim that individual verbs did not appear in multiple structures, Tomasello treated all single-argument utterances as being the same sort of structure on the grounds that children at this point in development cannot be assumed to have control over word order. Thus, "draw dog" (verb+noun) would not be considered different in grammatical structure from "I draw" (noun+verb). Applying the same analysis to the present data, we coded all 10 instances of our children's verb uses for whether they appeared in single argument frames or holophrastically, treating utterances with arguments in either the subject or object position as equivalent.

The results are shown in Table 13, together with data from Travis. We recoded Travis's data from the Appendix of Tomasello (1992), using only instances of the 34 target verbs of the present study. The data are not perfectly comparable because Tomasello did not consistently report all tokens of single verb use. This inconsistency, though, could only have the result of making Travis appear more, rather than less, grammatically advanced than the children in the present study. Higher percents indicate that

TABLE 13

PERCENT OF VERBS USED WITH ONE ARGUMENT OR IN
HOLOPHRASES

Child	%
Carl	79
Carrie	37
Elaine	84
Heather	52
Mae	53
Ned	86
Sam	90
Stacey	50
Travis	50

more verbs are "island like" or unproductive. The findings again reveal substantial variability: Applying Tomasello's coding to the subjects in the present study yields a picture in which four of the present participants demonstrate less flexibility than Travis, using over 75% of their verbs in single argument frames or in single-word utterances; three children look very similar to Travis, using about half of their verbs in single-argument or single-word utterances; only one child looks more flexible than Travis, using only 37% of her verbs in single-argument or single-word utterances. Thus, Travis does not appear to be an outlier on this dimension of verb use. According to Tomasello's criteria, seven of the eight children in the present study also appear to be in the "verb island" stage (see also McClure et al., 2006).

Beyond treating all single-argument utterances as the same grammatical structure, there is another aspect of Tomasello's procedure that leads, we would argue erroneously, to the conclusion that children are not productive in their early verb use. That is, Tomasello's analysis did not take into account the differing requirements of the individual verbs. His assessment of whether verbs are produced with multiple arguments and his inference of limited grammatical knowledge when they do not assume that the verbs all require multiple arguments. But they do not. In particular, intransitive verbs require only subjects; therefore, to view a child who uses subjects but not objects with *come* or *go* as "missing" arguments is inappropriate. Moreover, many of the verbs Tomasello regarded as transitive, such as *draw*, are in reality verbs that alternate between transitive and intransitive frames (Levin, 1993), such that the use of these verbs with just one argument is perfectly appropriate. For example, "I draw" can be a fully specified description if the context makes what is drawn obvious, and "draw dog" can be a fully specified command if the context makes the addressee obvious. The more revealing analysis, therefore, is to compare the children's argument use for each verb subclass (transitive, intransitive, alternating) to see if the children are using their arguments differently for the different subclasses.

Table 14 presents, by verb class, the percent of verb-containing utterances that are verb only, verb plus one argument (including subject, object, or source/goal arguments such as "look ball" and "go store," and disregarding word order), and verb plus two or more arguments. It is apparent in these data that the use of holophrases is high, particularly with intransitive and alternating verbs and that the frequency of one-argument frames is similar (approximately one third of all uses) for all three subclasses. However, as predicted, the use of two-argument frames is highest with the transitive and alternating verbs; moreover, the two-argument frame is as frequent as the one-argument frame for the transitive verbs. (Note that the seemingly anomalous 2-NP uses found with intransitive verbs arose because

63

TABLE 14

Child/Subclass	Holophrase	1 Argument[a]	2 Arguments[a]	3 Arguments[a]	Other[b]
			Frame Type		
Carl					
Transitive	0	40	70	0	0
Intransitive	64.3	27.14	0	na	8.6
Alternating	82.31	5.38	4.62	na	0
Carrie					
Transitive	0	10	85.5	4.44	0
Intransitive	14.44	64.44	10	na	11.11
Alternating	21.67	49.2	30.83	na	0
Elaine					
Transitive	45	20	35	0	0
Intransitive	57.14	42.85	0	na	0
Alternating	51	41	8	na	0
Heather					
Transitive	3.75	48.75	43.75	1.25	2.5
Intransitive	24.44	47.77	0	na	32.2
Alternating	25.38	50	22.31	na	10
Mae					
Transitive	12.22	24.44	35.56	11.11	5.56
Intransitive	70	11.25	12.5	na	6.25
Alternating	32.3	30.77	29.23	na	0
Ned					
Transitive	30	65	5	0	0
Intransitive	97	3	0	na	0
Alternating	77.14	10	0	na	12.85
Sam					
Transitive	42.2	41.1	6.67	0	10
Intransitive	50	31.43	4.3	na	14.3
Alternating	79.3	9.3	0	na	11.3
Stacey					
Transitive	2	66	32	0	0
Intransitive	47.1	42.9	0	na	10
Alternating	35	36.67	11.67	na	16.67
Travis					
Transitive	10	64	22	2	2
Intransitive	33	25	na	na	43
Alternating	14	78	3	na	6
Mean					
Transitive	16.89	39.41	39.19	2.1	2.26
Intransitive	53.05	33.85	3.35		10.31
Alternating	50.51	29.04	13.33		6.35

Note.—[a]Subjects, required objects, recipients, and locations.
[b]Adverbs, prepositions, vocative uses (e.g., "Mom, come").

of uses of *look* and *sit* that were missing their prepositions, e.g., "Grandma look doggie" and "Dolly sit chair.")

The critical question for the Verb Island Hypothesis is whether these data indicate systematic differences in the number of arguments appearing with subcategories of verbs that would be predicted on the basis of the adult grammar. If children's grammars are lexically based, then children have no category VERB and, by implication, no subcategories of verbs. If, however, children's very early verb uses show differences related to verb subclass, this implies the existence of underlying verb subclasses in children's linguistic representations. (Admittedly, from our data set, we do not know if these go beyond the input given.) This hypothesis was tested in a 3 (verb type) × 3 (number of arguments) repeated measures ANOVA, which yielded a significant interaction, $F(4, 28) = 7.46$, $p = .0005$. Pairwise contrasts using the Bonferroni correction ($p < .005$) revealed that within the intransitive verbs, holophrastic utterances were more frequent than either one- or two-argument utterances, $Fs(1, 7) > 17$, $ps < .004$, Cohen's $ds > 0.73$. Transitive verbs were used holophrastically with less frequency than either intransitive or alternating verbs, $Fs(1, 7) > 16$, $ps < .005$, $ds > 1.35$; the transitive verbs also tended to appear in significantly more two-argument frames than the intransitive verbs, $F(1, 7) = 15.22$, $p = .006$, $d = 1.72$. In sum, under the appropriate analysis, all of the children—even Travis—demonstrate knowledge of the difference in frames privileged by transitive and intransitive verbs from the beginning of their use of those verbs (see also Goldin-Meadow, 2003, and McClure et al., 2006, for similar findings).

The Manchester Corpus

The degree of syntactic flexibility observed in this study is also greater than that reported in Lieven and colleagues' studies of their Manchester corpus (Lieven et al., 2003; Pine et al., 1998; Theakston et al., 2001, 2004). Three findings, in particular, are at odds. First, the degree of lexical subject flexibility with intransitive verbs in our data is considerably higher than that reported by Pine et al. (1998); namely, 25% for their study, 36–52% for ours; see Table 12. Second, whereas Theakston et al. (2004; Table 8) reported syntactic flexibility on the order of two frames per verb in their children within, on average, 6 weeks (thus including many more instances of a given verb than we could), we find comparable numbers of flexibility within, on average, just over 2 weeks. It seems likely that we found more and earlier grammatical flexibility because the present data were, to use Lieven et al.'s term, "denser." That is, every instance produced by our children (within the first 10 for a given verb) was recorded; moreover, children's utterances were recorded across a wide range of situations. As discussed in chapter I, relying on situation-restricted sampled speech to make judgments concerning toddlers' grammatical productivity may yield underestimates of productivity.

Lieven et al. (2003; see also Lieven, 2006) make a further claim that is also relevant to the present analyses of the diary records. Lieven and colleagues have claimed that children's early verb+noun combinations are not indications of grammatical flexibility because a large number of these, in their corpus, involved substitution of only one word at a time. For example, saying "Doggie go" and then "Kitty go," or "Bring cooky" and then "Bring juice" does not count as flexibility to Lieven et al. because a change of only one word could simply indicate flexibility at the lexical rather than grammatical levels. In contrast, in the coding scheme used in the present study, both of the above examples would have been counted as changes (in lexical subject or object) and thus counted as indicators of flexibility. We have two counters to Lieven et al.'s interpretation of this type of flexibility. The first counterargument is practical: Children in the toddler years are at a stage of utterance production that is limited in terms of length; they only produce two to three words at a time (Bloom, 1973; Valian et al., 2006). Thus, if the verb stays the same, only one other word *could* change over the course of sequential utterances. Changes of one word at a time would be the only way these children could show syntactic flexibility, because of output constraints and not because of the absence of abstract grammar. Put another way, the finding that young children are limited in the number of words that can vary from one utterance to the next is a logical consequence of length limitations rather than an independent discovery regarding their grammatical knowledge.

The second counterargument comes directly from the diary records. As described earlier in this chapter, the children in the present study were more likely to change the frame entirely (i.e., demonstrate syntactic flexibility, which included adding or subtracting nouns, Ps, and/or negation) than to change the nouns in the frame (i.e., demonstrate lexical subject or lexical object flexibility). Moreover, individual children also demonstrated considerable grammatical flexibility that went beyond just changing nouns in a given frame. The first example of such flexibility comes from one of the "star" children, Heather. Early in her verb production, she said "I coming" and "Come here" within 30 days (starting at 18 months); to Lieven et al., this might be coded as just a one-word substitution and not real flexibility. However, she also said "Drop," "I drop," "I drop something," and "I dropped it" over the same span of time; these comprise multiple word changes. Moreover, at 23 months Heather said "take a bite," "I take bite," and "Take this" all in the same day, clearly showing syntactic flexibility. Furthermore, such demonstrations were not a property of only the "star" verb users: Carl was one of our slower learners, yet he also said "I no walk" followed by (on the same day) "Gavin walk," and "I don't like" followed by (on the same day) "I like cheese." Both of these couplets involved changes of more than one word, and thus would count for grammatical flexibility even on Lieven et al.'s criteria. As argued above, we believe that our children demonstrated more grammatical flexibility than those in the Manchester corpus because our data set includes speech from a wider range of situations/contexts. We would argue, in addition, that the coding scheme applied to the Manchester corpus (and that used by Tomasello) biases the results toward finding little grammatical productivity. That is, Lieven et al. and Tomasello claim to have discovered that children are not productive in their use of verbs. This discovery is not, however, independent of their coding decisions. Having decided to credit the child with little grammatical knowledge on an utterance-by-utterance basis, it is not surprising that they then find that the children demonstrate little grammatical knowledge in their speech overall.

CONCLUSIONS

In sum, the data presented in this chapter support our contention that American English learners—at least, the eight we have studied in such detail—demonstrate grammatical flexibility in their verb use from its very onset. Overwhelmingly, the first 10 instances of these 34 common verbs appear in multiple frames. Moreover, these first 10 uses show sensitivity to verb subclass, in that transitive verbs appear less frequently as holophrases and tend to appear more frequently than intransitive verbs in frames with two arguments. These data contradict descriptions of children's early verb use as restricted, with each verb appearing in its own limited range of syntactic environments. These data do not suggest an account of acquisition in which young language learners have underlying grammars in which each verb is an "island" unto itself. The data are more consistent with an account in which even very young learners are acquiring the grammatical patterns of their input language.

VI. DIFFERENCES IN EARLY VERB GROWTH AND USE AS A FUNCTION OF DEVELOPMENTAL PERIOD, CHILD, AND VERB

In chapter V, we presented analyses that revealed some grammatical productivity and flexibility in the first verb uses of eight children. All children used at least one syntactic frame with multiple verbs; three children used all five coded frames with multiple verbs. All the children used at least some of their first verbs with grammatical flexibility, and each of these early-acquired verbs was used flexibly by at least some children during the window of this study. Within that picture of early and pervasive flexibility, there was variability among children and among verbs in the degree of flexibility observed. It is also possible that there was variability across the duration of the study that has been unexplored in the analyses presented thus far. In this chapter, we examine differences among periods of development, among children, and among verbs in more detail, and we examine the interrelations among the measured properties of children's verb use to provide further tests of the theories of verb development we have considered.

DOES FLEXIBILITY OF VERB USE VARY BY PERIOD OF VERB DEVELOPMENT?

According to the conservative-child hypothesis described in chapter I, grammar is at first lexically specific; only later are the combinatorial possibilities of verbs represented in a grammar with an abstract category of VERB (MacWhinney, 2004; Ninio, 1999, 2007; Tomasello, 2000). The present findings, that most verbs are used with multiple frames and most frames used with multiple verbs within the first 10 instances of verb use, are inconsistent with this position. It is still possible, however, that there is a developmental progression in the abstractness of children's grammars such that verbs that are learned first are used with less flexibility than verbs that are learned later. To address this proposal, we go back to the data to test the hypothesis that there is an early stage of nonproductive verb use, suffi-

TABLE 15a

CHILDREN'S AGE (MONTHS) FOR EACH DEVELOPMENTAL PERIOD

	Child							
Period	Carl	Mae	Sam	Heather	Elaine	Carrie	Stacey	Ned
1	20–21	19–20	16–17	19–20	20–21	18–19	16–17	17–18
2 ends	23.5	22.5	19.5	22.5	23.5	21.5	19.5	20.5
3 ends	25.5	24.5	21.5	24.5	25.5	23.5	21.5	
4 ends	27.5	26.5	23.5	26.5				
5 end	29.5	28.5	25.5	28.5				
6 ends	31.5	30.5						
7 ends	33.5	32.5						

TABLE 15b

CHILDREN'S MLU FOR EACH DEVELOPMENTAL PERIOD

	Child							
Period	Carl	Mae	Sam	Heather	Elaine	Carrie	Stacey	Ned
1	1	1	1	1.98	2.18	2.68	1.65	1.17
2	1	1.05	1.2	2.58	1.71	3.95	2.71	2.06
3	1	2	1.15	3.67	2.7	4.37	3.08	
4	1.93	2.32	1.48	5.08				
5	2.52	3.31	2.3	3.8				
6	2.2	4.04						
7	3.45	5.72						

Note.—MLU = mean length of utterances.

ciently brief that it was obscured by the overall productive and flexible nature of verb use during the long window of this study.

We analyzed each child's verb use across his/her participation in the study. We divided each child's span of participation into developmental periods, as follows: Period 1 included each child's first 6 weeks of participation and thus, given the participant-selection requirements of the study, their very first verbs. Period 2 included each child's next 8 weeks of participation, Period 3 included the next 8 weeks, Period 4 included the subsequent 8 weeks, and so on to the end of their participation. Some children (Carl, Mae) participated through seven periods (see Table 15a), others (Sam, Heather) participated through five periods, others (Elaine, Carrie, Stacey) participated through three periods, and one (Ned) participated through two periods. It is important to point out that because we have records only for each child's first 10 uses of each verb, the later periods include data only from later-learned verbs and not from additional uses of

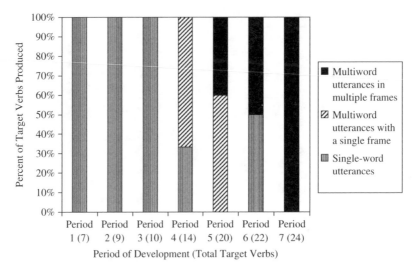

FIGURE 11.—The development of syntactic flexibility in newly learned verbs: Carl.

early-learned verbs. Thus, the crucial question concerns whether the first 10 instances of later-learned verbs consistently display more flexibility than the first 10 instances of early-learned verbs. Tables 15a and 15b present the children's ages and mean length of utterances (MLUs), respectively, for each of the periods in which they participated. The MLUs are estimates, calculated using only the verb-containing utterances recorded in the diaries.

Figures 11 through 18 present each child's timeline individually; Figure 19 presents all children in a single figure. The figures are ordered beginning with those children who participated for the greatest number of periods, Carl and Mae, and ending with Ned, who participated for the fewest periods. As shown in Figure 11, Carl began with seven verbs in his first period and added new verbs slowly during his next two periods. All of his verbs in these first three periods were in single-word utterances and hence not used grammatically flexibly (gray bars). During his fourth period, he began to use verbs in multiword utterances (striped bars); however, both verbs were only used in one frame (subject–verb [SV]). It was during his fifth period, when he was between 27.5 and 29.5 months of age, that he used two verbs both in multiword utterances *and* in different frames within the first 10 instances (black bars). The frames included SV, verb–object (VO), and SVO. Thus, Carl began to show grammatical flexibility during Period 5. Mae, shown in Figure 12, displayed a similar although not identical pattern. Mae began using two verbs in Period 1, then added eight more verbs in Period 2 but only eight more verbs in Period 3. Unlike Carl, throughout

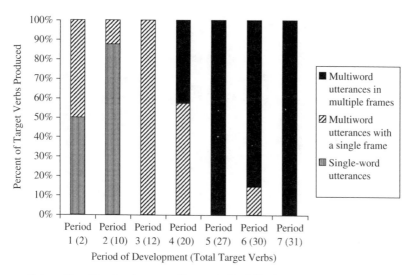

FIGURE 12.—The development of syntactic flexibility in newly learned verbs: Mae.

these three periods she used some verbs in multiword utterances within her first 10 instances. However, as was the case for Carl, each verb appeared in only one frame: During Period 1, one verb appeared with a preposition (P) and during periods 2 and 3, verbs appeared only in the SV frame. During Period 4 (i.e., one developmental period earlier than Carl), she used three verbs in multiword utterances *and* in different frames of multiword utterances within the first 10 instances. Frames of SV, VO, SVO, and verb–preposition (VP) were all represented. Mae thus began to show grammatical flexibility during Period 4, between 24.5 and 26.5 months of age. Sam, shown in Figure 13, also displayed this general pattern of (a) restricted use of his target verbs in multiword utterances for their first 10 instances during Periods 1–3 and then (b) mostly multiword use and multiframe use beginning at Period 4. At his Period 4, Sam used his verbs in the SV, VO, SVO, and VP frames. The timeline data from these three children (Carl, Mae, and Sam) provide some support for a weaker version of the conservative-child hypothesis: First verbs were produced in restricted frames (either single-word utterances or multiword utterances using only one frame); later verbs were produced in flexible frames.

However, not all of the children followed this pattern. Heather (Figure 14) and Carrie (Figure 15) demonstrated grammatical flexibility in their verb use starting at Period 1. Both girls produced many verbs even during their first 6 weeks of participation in the study ($n = 16$ and 13, respectively), and they used approximately half of these verbs in multiword utterances and in different frames within the first 10 instances during Period 1.

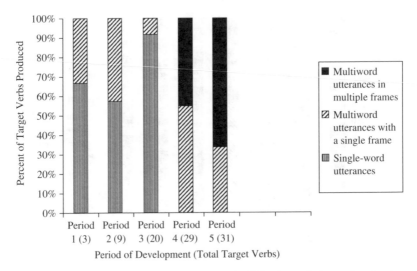

FIGURE 13.—The development of syntactic flexibility in newly learned verbs: Sam.

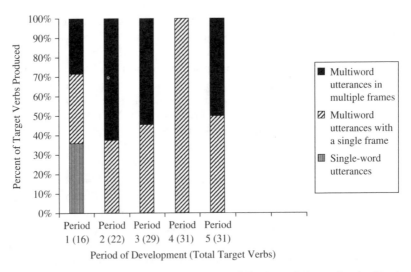

FIGURE 14.—The development of syntactic flexibility in newly learned verbs: Heather.

Heather and Carrie used the SV, VO, SVO, VP, and V-ing frames all during Period 1, and grammatically flexible use continued through each child's next two periods. Neither Carrie nor Heather provides any evidence of restricted verb use in terms of grammar, even for their very first verbs. They

72

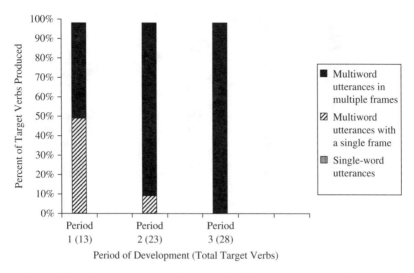

FIGURE 15.—The development of syntactic flexibility in newly learned verbs: Carrie.

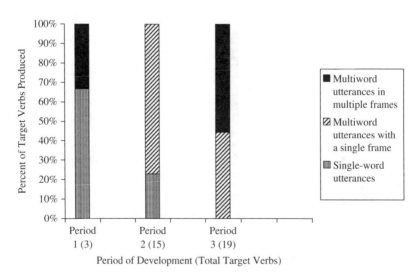

FIGURE 16.—The development of syntactic flexibility in newly learned verbs: Elaine.

also reached the ending point of the study more quickly than two of the three conservative-first children.

Elaine, Stacey, and Ned (Figures 16–18, respectively) may be considered "intermediate" with respect to their speed of reaching grammatical

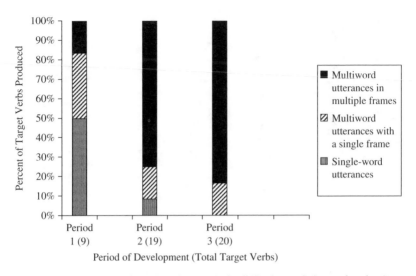

FIGURE 17.—The development of syntactic flexibility in newly learned verbs: Stacey.

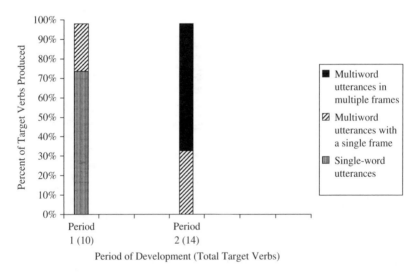

FIGURE 18.—The development of syntactic flexibility in newly learned verbs: Ned.

flexibility of verb use: Each used 1 verb in multiple frames within the first 10 instances during Period 1. Elaine and Stacey both used their one multiframe verb during Period 1 in the SV, VO, and SVO frames. Also during this period, Stacey used two additional verbs in just one multiword frame within the first 10 instances (Elaine used none in this way). Leaps in grammatical flexibility were then displayed during Period 2 (Stacey) or Period 3 (Elaine).

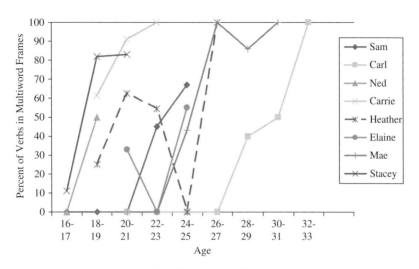

FIGURE 19.—Change in multiword use by age.

Thus, they showed earlier flexibility than Carl, Mae, or Sam; however, their flexibility was not displayed across as wide a number of verbs as was Carrie's or Heather's. Ned participated for the fewest periods and, like Carl, Sam, and Mae, used his first 10 verbs in only restricted single-word or multiword utterances for their first 10 instances during Period 1. During Period 2, though, he produced four new verbs and used two of them in multiword utterances and in different frames within the first 10 instances. Ned's frames during Period 2 included SV, VO, and SVO.

The different pathways to grammatical flexibility that these children demonstrated can be seen together in Figure 19. Figure 19 displays the cumulative *percent* of verbs produced in multiword utterances in different frames within the first 10 instances for each child across periods. As the figure shows, Carrie, Stacy, Elaine, Heather, and Ned produced considerable multiword utterances in different frames during Periods 2 and 3, whereas Sam, Mae, and Carl reached these levels only during Periods 4–6 of their verb use.

This analysis of individual children's developmental changes in the grammatical flexibility with which they used newly acquired verbs reveals that the majority of the children, although not all children, showed grammatical flexibility close to the very onset of verb use. Moreover, even the child who was slowest to achieve grammatical flexibility, Carl, displayed such flexibility before the age of 2.5 years; Sam, another "slow" learner, actually demonstrated grammatical flexibility before 24 months of age. Heather, Stacy, Ned, and Carrie demonstrated grammatical flexibility before 20 months of age. Both these developmental patterns and the ages of the first grammatical flexibility demonstration are at odds with those reported by other researchers, who have claimed that there is little grammatical flexibility until children are close to 2.5 years of age and that children's initial use of sentence frames is predominantly, if not exclusively, verb specific (e.g., MacWhinney, 2004; McClure et al., 2006; Tomasello, 2000, p. 213).

ARE LIGHT VERBS PATHBREAKERS TO GRAMMATICAL FLEXIBILITY?

Previous comparisons of the grammatical environments surrounding light and heavy verbs in children's first verb uses (in chapters III and V) revealed that light verbs appeared significantly more frequently with direct objects and in SVO frames than heavy verbs and that light verbs appeared significantly earlier and more frequently with different direct objects than did heavy verbs. These findings might be considered evidence for the claim that light verbs function as facilitators of children's acquisition of abstract phrase–level sentence frames (Chenu & Jisa, 2006; E. Clark, 1987; Goldberg, 1999; Goldberg & Casenhiser, 2006; Ninio, 1999, 2005a, 2005b; Pinker, 1989; Rice & Bode, 1993) because the light verbs, among the target verbs in this study, did seem—overall—to show more and earlier direct object flexibility. However, the finding of greater flexibility for light verbs was limited to the direct object slot; light verbs did not show greater grammatical flexibility overall (Table 14). Furthermore, light verbs may have appeared with more, earlier, and more varied direct objects not because of any syntactic privilege but because the meanings of light verbs are general and thus expressing the direct objects is necessary for communicative purposes to sufficiently specify the event or relation that the child is talking about (e.g., Snedeker & Gleitman, 2004; Theakston et al., 2004).

It is possible, however, that these averaged data missed potential pathbreaking functions that individual light verbs might have served for individual children. As listed in Table 1, the light verbs among the target verbs in this study were fairly diverse, and some of these (go, put, want) have figured more heavily in proposals of the pathbreaker hypothesis than others (Chenu & Jisa, 2006; Goldberg, 1999; Goldberg & Casenhiser, 2006; Ninio, 1999). The following analyses investigated such potential functions for each child individually, considering each light verb that each child produced. Following Theakston et al. (2004), we investigated whether individual light verbs participated in a wider range of different frames than verbs with more specific meanings that were acquired at the same age. We compared the frame flexibility of each light verb with (a) the heavy verb that appeared just

TABLE 16

CARL'S LIGHT/HEAVY VERB COMPARISON FOR FRAME FLEXIBILITY

Preceding Verb(s)	Light Verb	Following Verb(s)	Age (Days)		Number of Frames Used in 10 Instances (Frame)	Examples
			1st Use	10th Use		
Push			658	680	1 (V)	Push
	GO		680	680	1 (V)	Go
		Kiss	715	715	1 (V)	Kiss
Sit			808	808	2 (SV, noV)	Me sit, No sit
Cry			800	800	2 (V, SV)	Cry, Baby cry
	COME		814	814	1 (V)	Come
		Cut	827	827	3 (V, VO, SV)	Cut, Cut paper, Mama cut
Cut			827	827	3 (V, VO, SV)	Cut, Cut paper, Mama cut
	GIVE		828	828	2 (VIO, SVIO)	Give me, Sissy give me
		Hold	861	861	1 (SVO)	I hold (flash)light
Cut			827	827	3 (V, VO, SV)	Cut, Cut paper, Mama cut
	LOOK		838	840	2 (V, V locative)	Look, Look punch bag
		Hold	861	861	1 (SVO)	I hold (flash)light
Like			911	911	2 (SVO, SV-neg O)	I don't like, I like cheese
	WANT		928	932	2 (SVO, SV+S)	Me want it, Me want to do it
		Wash	932	932	3 (SVO, VO, V)	Me wash table, Wash floor, Wash

Note.—V = Verb; S = subject; SV = subject–verb; VO = verb–object; SVO = subject–verb–object. Capitalized verbs are highlighted relative to "regular" verbs.

before this light verb's first use and (b) the heavy verb that appeared just after this light verb's first use. We also looked across the range of earliest verbs used by each child to see which verb(s) first appeared with which frames. Given that our data set was verb centered rather than frame centered, though, we are unable to address the related question of whether the very first uses of a frame appeared with light verbs. The findings are presented in Tables 16–23, described below in detail for Carl and summarized for the rest of the children.

Carl produced six light verbs. Each was preceded in development by a heavy, more specific verb (see Table 16), and none of the light verbs was more flexible in its use than the just-preceding heavy verb. Moreover, light verbs were not consistently the first ones to be produced in new constructions. For example, *cry*, produced at 800 days, was Carl's 13th verb but the first verb used with a subject. *Cut* was the first one used with an object, and *hold* was the first one used in the SVO frame. Carl's light verbs were the first to be used in the verb+locative (VL) (inchoative motion) and VOL (caused motion) frames/constructions; however, his "first-in-frame" light verbs were

TABLE 17
CARRIE's LIGHT/HEAVY VERB COMPARISON FOR FRAME FLEXIBILITY

Preceding Verb(s)	Light Verb	Following Verb(s)	Age (Days)		Number of Frames Used in 10 Instances (Frame)	Examples
			1st Use	10th Use		
Push			564	574	3 (V, SV, VO)	Push, Arty push, Push mommy
Wash			565	583	3 (V, SV, VO)	Wash, I wash, Wash my hands
	GO		568	582	3 (V, V L, SVL)	Go, Go bye-bye, Daddy go work
		Walk	569	644	3 (V, SV, SV-ing)	Walk, Mom walk, Doggie walking
Cry			590	601	2 (SV, SV-ing)	Baby cry, Arty crying
	COME		593	603	2 (V, SV-ing)	Come, Granny coming
		Run	594	603	2 (SV, SV-ing)	Arty run, My running
Open			585	600	3 (V, SV, VO)	Open, Open teeth, Daddy open
	WANT		593	626	1 (SVO)	I want my daddy
		Kiss	595	616	3 (no V, SV, VO)	No kiss, Kiss baby, Daddy kiss
Hold			604	622	3 (SVO, neg, -ing)	No Mom hold it, Daddy holding it
	LOOK		608	625	2 (V, V locative)	Look, Look my shoe
		Pull	622	660	3 (SVO, neg, -ing)	No pull my shirt, Daddy pulling it
See			628	660	1 (SVO)	My see doggie
	PUT		644	670	1 (SVO)	Mommy put shoes
		Need	652	679	1 (SVO)	My need my binka
Need			652	679	1 (SVO)	My need my binka
	BRING		659	683	1 (SVO)	I bring my baby
		Wave	672	691	3 (SV, SVIO, SVing)	Dad wave, I wave at A, My waving
Need			652	679	1 (SVO)	My need my binka
	TAKE		659	681	3 (Neg VO, SVO, NegSVO)	No take it, No my take my nap, Daddy take my sippy
		Wave	672	691	3 (SV, SVIO, SVing)	Dad wave, I wave at A, My waving
Roll			687	709	3 (SVO, SVP, SVing)	My roll my hands, Wagon rolling down, all rolling
	GIVE		690	708	3 (VOP, SVOIO, VO)	Give mom hug, I give my cookie to A, Give that back
	No verbs were produced after Give					

Note.— V = Verb; S = subject; SV = subject–verb; VO = verb–object; SVO = subject–verb–object. Capitalized verbs are highlighted relative to irregular verbs.

not the ones predicted: *Look* was his first verb to be used in the VL frame (*look punch bag*) instead of the predicted *go*, and *give* was his first verb used in the V(O)L frame (*give me*) instead of the predicted *put*. Admittedly, given the time elapsed between Carl's 10th production of *go* and his 1st production of

TABLE 18

ELAINE's Light/Heavy Verb Comparison for Frame Flexibility

Preceding Verb(s)	Light Verb	Following Verb(s)	Age (Days) 1st Use	10th Use	Number of Frames Used in 10 Instances (Frame)	Examples
	WANT		602	613	1 (SVO)	I want veggies
	GO		613	710	2 (V, SV)	Go, I go
	LOOK		633	634	1 (V)	Look
		Open	651	651	1 (V)	Open
		Sit	653	656	1 (SV)	I sit
		See	658	672	2 (V, SV)	See, I see
Roll			695	716	1 (V)	Roll
	COME		696	716	3 (V, VV, SV)	Come, Come roll, My come
		Wash	696	741	2 (SVO, VO)	I wash hands, Wash hands

Note.— V = Verb; S = subject; SV = subject–verb; VO = verb–object; SVO = subject–verb–object. Capitalized verbs are highlighted relative to "regular" verbs.

look, it is probably not the case that his VL production with *look* was his very first in that frame; however, this caveat does not hold for his 1st production of a verb in the VOL frame. That is, when Carl produced *give me* he had not yet produced even one instance of *put*, *bring*, or *take*; therefore, it is very likely that *give me* was one of his first, if not his very first, use of the VOL frame.

Carrie, Ned, and Heather each showed a similar pattern to Carl's, in that (a) none of their light verbs was used more flexibly than concurrently produced heavy verbs and (b) only some frames were used first with light verbs, whereas others were used first with heavy verbs (Tables 17, 19, and 21). For Mae, Sam, and Stacey, some proportion (one quarter to two thirds) of their light verbs were used more flexibly than their concurrently produced heavy verbs; however, they were no more likely to produce specific frames first with the predicted light verbs (e.g., VL with *go* or VOL with *put*) (Tables 20, 22, and 23). Note that the first 10 uses of *make* were (voluntarily) recorded by Mae's and Stacey's mothers; *make* has been proposed as a pathbreaker verb for the VO frame, yet it was neither the earliest nor the most flexible verb in this frame for either child. In fact, only Elaine followed the predicted pattern, such that both her first uses of grammatical forms and her first flexible uses of such forms appeared with light verbs (Table 18). These data, then, corroborate those of Theakston et al. (2004), who found no consistent advantage in grammatical flexibility for light verbs at this early point in development.

Table 24 presents a summary for seven commonly appearing frames, whether they were first used by the children with light or with heavy verbs. Clearly, there is no consistent advantage for the light verbs here either, as heavy verbs were the pathbreakers at least as frequently for the S, O, -ing,

TABLE 19

HEATHER's LIGHT/HEAVY VERB COMPARISON FOR FRAME FLEXIBILITY

Preceding Verb(s)	Light Verb	Following Verb(s)	Age (Days) 1st Use	10th Use	Number of Frames Used in 10 Instances (Frame)	Examples
Cut			584	629	2 (VO, SVO)	Cut this, I cut this
	GO		585	590	1 (V)	Go
		Sit	585	590	1 (V P)	Sit down
Sit			585	590	1 (V P)	Sit down
	COME		593	634	2 (SV-ing, V locative)	I coming, Come here
		Drop	595	629	4 (V, SV, SVO, SVedO)	Drop, I dropped it, I drop
Kiss			589	708	4 (V, SVO, VO, SV)	I kiss it, Mommy kiss, Kiss that
	PUT		593	701	4 (V, V locative, SVP, VOP)	Put here, Put top on, I put on
		Push	588	600	2 (V, VO)	Push, Push this
		Drop	595	629	4 (V, SV, SVO, SVedO)	Drop, I dropped it, I drop
Wash			593	652	2 (VO, V)	Wash, Wash it
	WANT		595	624	2 (SVO, SV+negO)	I want it, I don't want this
		Like	611	615	2 (VO, SVO)	Like this, I like this
Need			618	631	2 (VO, SVO)	Me need this, need this
	LOOK		633	653	2 (V, V locative)	Look, Look here
		Eat	634	652	3 (V, SV, SVO)	Eat, Heather eat, Heather eat this
Throw			669	701	5 (SVO, SV, V P, SVP SVOP)	I throw that, throw away I threw down, I throw it away
	GIVE		687	708	5 (VO, VIO, VPP, SVPP SVOPP)	M give it, Give me, Give to D, A gave to me A gave coin to me
	TAKE		701	701	2 (VO, SVO)	Take a bite, Daddy take this
		Wave	702	827	3 (V bye, V PP VL)	Wave bye, We need to wave to D, I waved M
		Stop	710	710	1 (V+gerund)	Stop eating the flowers

Note.— V = Verb; S = subject; SV = subject–verb; VO = verb–object; SVO = subject–verb–object. Capitalized verbs are highlighted relative to "regular" verbs.

and P frames. Some frames did consistently first appear with light verbs; however, the pathbreaking verbs that were observed were not consistently the ones predicted. That is, a light verb *was* consistently the first one used for the VL frame; however, for only two children (Carrie, Stacey) was this, as predicted, *go*. For the other four children, the pathbreaker was *come* (one child) or *look* (three children). Similarly, a light verb was consistently used first in the VOL frame, but for only one child (Heather) this was the predicted *put*. For the other five children, the pathbreaker was *give* (two), *take* (two), or *bring* (one). Finally, *want*, a stative rather than action verb, was the first verb produced in the SVO frame for six of our children; *need*, another

TABLE 20

MAE's Light/Heavy Verb Comparison for Frame Flexibility

Preceding Verb(s)	Light Verb	Following Verb(s)	Age (Days) 1st Use	10th Use	Number of Frames Used in 10 Instances (Frame)	Examples
Push			577	589	1 (V)	Push
	COME		616	625	1 (V on)	Come on
		Throw	624	630	1 (V)	Throw
Eat			654	669	1 (V)	Eat
	GO		661	684	1 (V)	Push
		Fall	673	756	2 (V, SV)	Fall, Mommy fall
Run			731	750	2 (V, VP)	Run, Run away
Cut			740	819	3 (V, SV, VO)	Cut, Me cut, Cut it
	LOOK		757	757	1 (V loc)	Look me
		Cry	742	776	3 (V, SV, V-neg)	Cry, Jill cry, Don't cry
		Pull	765	898	5 (VO, VOP, SVOP SVO)	Pull feet, This one pull off, Me pull it over, Me pull it
Open			727	733	3 (V, SV, VO)	Open, Mommy open, Open this
	WANT		769	838	3 (SVO, VOS-bar, VO)	Me want cheese, Want Panda watch me, I want that
		Pull	765	898	5 (VO, VOP, SVOP, SVO)	Pull feet, This one pull off, Me pull it over, Me pull it
Hold			773	777	2 (SVO, SV)	Me hold her, Me hold
	BRING		791	834	1 (SVO)	Me bring rock
Need			789	820	3 (VO, SVO, NegVO)	Me need that, No need that plate
	TAKE		795	863	3 (VOP, SVOP, SVO)	Take that off, Me take my pie out, I take it
Drop			802	818	2 (SVO, VO)	Drop my Teddy, Me drop my Bandaid
	PUT		812	856	4 (VP, VOP, VOPP, SVPP)	Put on, Put me over, Put me up Jill's table
		Like	833	910	2 (SVO, S-neg VO)	I like that, I don't like pears
Like			833	910	2 (SVO, S-neg VO)	I like that, I don't like pears
	GIVE		840	928	3 (SVO, SVOIO, SVOPP)	Me give my ring to Jill, Me give Jill a toy
	MAKE		851	880	3 (VO, SVO, past)	I made, Me made tower
		Wash	855	868	2 (SVO, VO)	Me wash it, wash my hands

Note.— V = Verb; S = subject; SV = subject–verb; VO = verb–object; SVO = subject–verb–object. Capitalized verbs are highlighted relative to "regular" verbs.

desire verb, was the SVO pathbreaker for the seventh child, and *cut* or *hold* for the eighth.

The finding that the particular light verb used first in a frame varied across children is contrary to two crucial parts of the light-verbs-as-pathbreakers

TABLE 21

NED's Light/Heavy Verb Comparison for Frame Flexibility

Preceding Verb(s)	Light Verb	Following Verb(s)	Age (Days) 1st Use	Age (Days) 10th Use	Number of Frames Used in 10 Instances (Frame)	Examples
Roll			519	549	2 (V, Ving)	Roll, Rolling
	COME		526	549	2 (V, V P)	Come, Come on
		Bite	526	580	1 (V)	Bite
		Lay	549	568	2 (V, V P)	Lay, lay down, lay back
Like			556	611	2 (V, VO)	Like, Like it
	WANT		578	593	1 (VO)	Want some
		Need	580	615	2 (VO, SVO)	Need a cookie, Pop needs a pen

Note.—V = Verb; S = subject; VO = verb–object; SVO = subject–verb–object. Capitalized verbs are highlighted relative to "regular" verbs.

hypothesis. One part of the hypothesis targets the pathbreaking verb's *transparency of meaning*, which is proposed to enable children to conceive of or to abstract the frames (Goldberg, 1999; Goodman & Sethuraman, 2006). That is, children learn how *go* encodes inchoative motion, or *put* encodes caused motion, or *make* involves caused action, and then deduce from the verb's meaning that *go* is to be followed by locatives, *make* is to be followed by object names, and *put* is to be followed by object names and locatives. From these "semantic frames," they abstract the grammatical frames VL (or VPP), VO, and VOL (or VOPP). *Bring*, *take*, *give*, and *put* might all be considered equally representative of the caused motion construction VOL, such that the variation here is not particularly problematic. However, *look* could not possibly be considered a transparent representative of the inchoative motion construction VL, because *look* involves a more abstract sense of motion, with someone's *gaze* being directed toward a ground rather than an object or person actually moving toward a ground (Landau & Gleitman, 1985; Levin, 1993). Mae's and Sam's innovative use of the VL frame first with *look* seems inexplicable in terms of an argument based on semantically transparent underpinnings.

The children's variability with the SVO frame pathbreaking verbs is similarly problematic for the light-verbs-as-pathbreakers hypothesis: If semantic transparency of transitive action is the instigator of children's abstraction of the SVO frame, then *want* hardly qualifies; as Hopper and Thompson (1980) and others have discussed at length, verbs such as *make* or *push*, which capture caused changes of state or position, are better candidates. Ninio (1999) and others (e.g., Theakston et al., 2004) have already grappled with the inconsistency of verbs like *want* appearing so early in the SVO frame

TABLE 22

SAM'S LIGHT/HEAVY VERB COMPARISON FOR FRAME FLEXIBILITY

Preceding Verb(s)	Light Verb	Following Verb(s)	Age (Days) 1st Use	Age (Days) 10th Use	Number of Frames Used in 10 Instances (Frame)	Examples
Open			495	566	1 (V)	Open
	GO		531	567	2 (SV, V)	Go, I go
		Cut	540	583	1 (V)	Cut
Cut			540	583	1 (V)	Cut
	LOOK		553	592	1 (VPP)	Look at me
		Eat	569	660	1 (V)	Eat
Eat			569	660	1 (V)	Eat
	COME		576	602	1 (V)	Come
		Hold	571	607	1 (V)	Hold
Drop			602	783	4 (V, SV, VO, VPP)	M drop, Drop diaper, Drop in tub
	WANT		632	722	3 (SVO, VO, SVS-bar)	I want cup, Want cup, I want to go
		Roll	644	711	2 (V, VO)	Roll ball, Roll
Drop			602	783	4 (V, SV, VO, VPP)	M drop, Drop diaper, Drop in tub
	TAKE		634	663	1 (V)	Take
		Roll	644	711	2 (V, VO)	Roll ball, Roll
Need			646	674	2 (VO, SV)	I need, Need this
	BRING		664	739	4 (VO, VOP, negV, Ving	Bring that, Bring my plate over, No bring, Bringing
		Like	673	705	3 (V, VO, negVO)	Like those, M like, Don't like you
Lay			679	739	3 (SV, SVP, SVPP)	Teddy lay, Lay down, Lay down with me
	PUT		694	732	2 (V P, VOP)	Put away, Put that back
		Run	697	750	5 (V, Ving, SVPP, SV, VPP)	Running, I run in water

Note.— V = Verb; S = subject; SV = subject–verb; VO = verb–object; SVO = subject–verb–object. Capitalized verbs are highlighted relative to "regular" verbs.

but not encoding highly transitive actions, and they have proposed different resolutions. Ninio (1999) suggested that an even more abstract ("prototypical") notion of transitivity, in which the subject's/agent's relation is more prominent, facilitates children's abstraction of the SVO frame, and Ned's use of *need* fits this notion. However, Carl's use of *cut* does not (*cut* clearly changes the patient and is more similar to the Hopper and Thompson version); thus, there is still individual variation unaccounted for.

TABLE 23

STACEY'S LIGHT/HEAVY VERB COMPARISON FOR FRAME FLEXIBILITY

Preceding Verb(s)	Light Verb	Following Verb(s)	Age (Days)		Number of Frames Used in 10 Instances (Frame)	Examples
			1st Use	10th Use		
Sit			491	529	1 (V)	Sit
	GO		491	498	2 (Wh SV, V)	Where Nanny go? Go
		Eat	495	624	5 (V, Ving, SVing, SVO, VingO)	Eat pizza, I'm eating, I eat it
Open			503	533	1 (V)	Open
	WANT		512	611	2 (VO, SVO)	I want juice, Want some more
		Run	516	611	2 (Ving, SVing)	Running, Girl running
Open			503	533	1 (V)	Open
	COME		518	600	3 (V, V P, SV P)	Come in, You come out
	TAKE		520	595	2 (VO, VOP)	Take it, Take it off
Hold			540	593	2 (VO, SVO)	Hold that duck, I hold this
	LOOK		572	621	2 (V, V PP)	Look, Look in mirror
		Jump	559	584	4 (Ving, SVing, SVed, V)	Kitty jumping, Kitty jumped
Wash			555	581	2 (SVing, VO)	Mommy's washing, Wash my hands
	PUT		572	598	1 (VOP)	Put it on, Put phone back
MAKE			598	675 (5th)	3 (SVO, VO, -ing)	Daddy make it, making messes

Note.— V = Verb; S = subject; SV = subject–verb; VO = verb–object; SVO = subject–verb–object. Capitalized verbs are highlighted relative to "regular" verbs.

The second part of the light-verbs-as-pathbreakers hypothesis, and potential resolution of the inconsistency between the hypothesis and the data, is that children's abstraction of grammatical frames is highly dependent on the frequency with which particular light verbs appear in a variety of frames in the input. That is, an alternative process of abstraction is that after children learn how *go* encodes inchoative motion, or *put* encodes caused motion, or *make* involves caused action, they next observe that *go* is frequently followed by locatives, *make* (or *want*) is frequently followed by object names, and *put* is frequently followed by object names and locatives. Then, over numerous hearings of these verbs with a wide variety of locatives and object names in the relevant positions in the input, the children abstract the VL (or VPP), VO, and VOL (or VOPP) frames. This latter procedure does not rely on the meaning of the verb to enable the abstraction but does rely on the frequent appearance (with varied lexical items) of a single verb in a given frame

TABLE 24

FIRST USES OF GRAMMATICAL FORMS BY VERB SUBCLASS FOR EACH CHILD

Grammatical Form	Child First Use With a Light Verb	First Use With a Heavy Verb
SV	Carrie, Heather, Sam, Stacey Elaine*	Carl, Carrie, Mae, Ned
VO	Heather*, Elaine*	Carl, Carrie, Mae, Ned, Sam, Stacey
SVO	Carrie*, Elaine*, Heather*, Mae* Sam*, Stacey*	Carl, Ned
"-ing"	Carrie	Heather
VP	Sam, Stacey, Ned (*come*)	Carrie, Heather, Mae, Ned (*lay*)
VL	Carl (*look*), Carrie (*go*), Heather (*come*) Mae (*look*), Sam (*look*), Stacey (*go*)	
VOL	Carl (*give*), Carrie (*give*), Heather (*put*) Mae (*take*), Sam (*bring*), Stacey (*take*)	

Note.—*Child's first use was with the verb *want*.

V = Verb; S = subject; SV = subject–verb; VO = verb–object; SVO = subject–verb–object.

(e.g., Casenhiser et al., 2003; Chenu & Jisa, 2006; Goldberg, 1999; Goodman & Sethuraman, 2006; Kidd, Lieven, & Tomasello, 2006; Theakston et al., 2004).

This frequency-based procedure does indeed account for the predominance of *want* as the children's pathbreaker for the SVO frame; however, it encounters difficulties in accounting for the occurrences of *look* or *come* as Mae's, Heather's, and Sam's pathbreakers for the VL frame, because *look* and *come* are much less frequent verbs than *go* in children's input and output (Naigles & Hoff-Ginsberg, 1998). Moreover, the highly differential frequencies of *put*, *bring*, *take*, and *give* (*put* appears approximately 2.5–3 times more frequently than the other verbs; Goldberg, 1999; Naigles & Hoff-Ginsberg, 1998) in corpora of caregivers' and children's speech make this process less viable as an explanation of children's acquisition of the VOL frame/construction: If *put* is so frequent in the VOL construction, why do Sam, Stacey, Carrie, Mae, and Carl all use other verbs with their first VOL frame?

In other words, the semantic transparency–based version of the light-verbs-as-pathbreakers hypothesis may account for the children's first uses of the VOL construction, but it does not account for their first uses of the VL and SVO frames. The frequency-based version of this hypothesis may account for the children's first uses of the SVO frame, but it has difficulties accounting for their first uses of the VL and VOL frames. Our data, then, do not support the pathbreaking-verbs hypothesis as a process by which children learn to abstract sentence frames.

According to generativist theories, the abstract grammar that underlies language productivity is autonomous, yielding the prediction that children's development of grammatical flexible verb use should be unrelated to the development of semantically flexible verb use or to the growth of a verb lexicon (e.g., Chomsky, 1981). Other theories of verb development, including theories that grammatical development results from domain-general learning processes, theories that grammar emerges from the lexicon, and the syntactic bootstrapping hypothesis, predict that the acquisition of a verb lexicon, the development of semantically flexible verb use, and the development of grammatically flexible verb use should all be positively related across children. The syntactic bootstrapping hypothesis additionally predicts that the grammatical flexibility with which different verbs are used should be related to the semantic flexibility with which those verbs are used because semantic understanding of a verb is based on syntactic analysis of that verb's environments.

One way to investigate these hypotheses with the current data might be to compare the degree and onset of flexibility demonstrated by the children in the different domains. Although it is not a given that our measures of pragmatic, semantic, and syntactic flexibility are so directly comparable (i.e., is a change in actor of the same magnitude as a change in syntactic frame?), we performed pairwise t tests between addressee, actor, affected object, and syntactic flexibility using four indices of flexibility (percent of children, number of instances, number of days, percent of verbs) and the Bonferroni correction to set alpha at .0083. Of all 16 comparisons, only 1 reached significance: Children were significantly more flexible with their affected object use than with their syntactic frame use, $t(7) = 4.83$, $p = .0018$. Importantly, *none* of the time-related comparisons reached significance, providing no evidence for the notion that flexibility in one domain emerges earlier than in another.

A better way to address these proposals, we feel, is to examine intercorrelations among properties of verb development and use. To reduce the number of correlations calculated, we focused on selected measures of descriptive and theoretical interest, and, where possible, we created composite scales.

INTERCORRELATIONS AMONG MEASURES OF CHILDREN'S VERB DEVELOPMENT AND USE

Composite measures were created to index the age at which the children started to use verbs and the semantic and grammatical flexibility of

TABLE 25

INTERCORRELATIONS AMONG MEASURES OF CHILDREN'S VERB DEVELOPMENT AND USE ($N = 8$ FOR ALL ANALYSES)

	1.	2.	3.	4.	5.	6.
1. Age verb use begins	—	−.670*	.042	−.527[+]	−.456	−.189
2. Semantic flexibility composite		—	.624*	.749**	.110	.586[+]
3. Grammatical flexibility composite			—	.537[+]	−.222	.796**
4. Number of verbs at 21 months				—	−.119	.839**
5. Number of frames at 21 months					—	−.183
6. Number of productive frames at 24 months						—

Note.— [+]$p < .10$ (one-tailed), *$p < .05$ (one-tailed), **$p < .01$ (one-tailed).

their first 10 uses of early-acquired verbs. The scales were created as follows: *Age at which verb use begins* was the average of two measures—the age of first verb use and the mean age of first use of all the target verbs the child used in the window of this study. Cronbach's α for this scale was .75. *Semantic flexibility of verb use* was the average of three measures: the percent of verbs used with different actors, the percent of verbs used with different affected objects, and the percent of verbs used to refer to different actions (Cronbach's α = .89). *Grammatical flexibility of verb use* was indexed by the average of four measures: percent of verbs used with different frames (excluding vocatives), percent of verbs used with different morphology, percent of verbs used with different lexical subjects, and percent of verbs used with different lexical objects (Cronbach's α = .87). We also included two snap-shot measures of children's verb lexicons and verb grammars at 21 months, which was the oldest age at which we have data for all participants: the number of target verbs in the child's vocabulary and the number of frames (out of 5: SV, VO, SVO, VP, V-ing) in the child's utterances. Last, we counted the number of productive frames each child had at 24 months, employing the 5-verbs-per-frame criterion. For each correlation, we expected that if the measures were related they would be positively related, except that age would yield a negative correlation because a younger age at the beginning of verb use is a positive indicator of verb development; therefore, all significance tests were one-tailed. The correlation matrix is presented in Table 25.

The correlations among measures of children's verb use in Table 25 reveal that children who began verb use at a younger age showed more semantic flexibility in their first verb uses, and they also tended to have larger verb vocabularies at 21 months compared with children who began verb use at an older age. The semantic flexibility with which children used their first verbs was also significantly related to the grammatical flexibility of their verb use, to the size of their verb vocabularies at 21 months, and (marginally) to the number of productive frames they had at 24 months.

TABLE 26

INTERCORRELATIONS AMONG VERBS' PROPERTIES OF USE IN EARLY CHILD SPEECH (NUMBER
OF VERBS IN ANALYSIS)

	1.	2.	3.	4.	5.
1. Age of onset	—	$-.277^+$	.122	$-.036$	.336*
		(28)	(34)	(25)	(34)
2. Percent children using to refer to different actions		—	.100	$.373^+$	$-.294^+$
			(28)	(19)	(28)
3. Percent children using with different actors			—	$-.020$	.349*
				(25)	(34)
4. Percent children using with different affected objects				—	$.307^+$
					(25)
5. Grammatical flexibility of use composite					—

Note.—$^+p<.10$ (one-tailed), *$p<.05$ (one-tailed).

The size of children's verb vocabularies at 21 months showed a marginally
significant positive correlation with overall grammatical flexibility of their
first verb uses and a significant positive correlation with the number of
productive frames they had at 24 months. The grammatical flexibility of
children's verb use also was positively related to children's number of productive frames at 24 months, suggesting that flexibility of use is, in fact, a
good index of grammatical productivity.

INTERCORRELATIONS AMONG MEASURES OF VERBS' DEVELOPMENT AND USE

To analyze the intercorrelations among properties of verbs, as they are
first used in children's speech, a composite measure of *grammatical flexibility*
was created by averaging four measures: the percent of children using the
verb with more than one frame, with more than one morphological inflection, with more than one lexical subject, and with more than one lexical
object (Cronbach's $\alpha = .79$). The multiple indices of semantic flexibility did
not form an internally consistent scale—as Table 26 shows, the three indices
of semantic flexibility were not significantly related to each other. Thus, the
following three measures were entered into analysis individually: the percent of children using the verb to refer to more than one action, the percent
of children using the verb with more than one actor, and the percent of
children using the verb with more than one affected object. The final measure of how verbs appear in children's speech was the average age at which
the verb first appeared. As was the case for the by child correlations, the
predictions were that positive indicators would be positively related, and all

significance tests were one-tailed. The correlation matrix is presented in Table 26.

The correlations among measures of how verbs were used within these first instances of children's verb production show that later-appearing verbs (i.e., verbs with an older age of onset) tended to be used by fewer children to refer to varied actions and were used by significantly more children with grammatical flexibility There were also trends toward the number of children using a verb to refer to multiple actions being positively associated with the number of children using that verb to refer to different affected objects and negatively associated with the number of children showing grammatical flexibility of use. Verbs used by more children with different actors were also used by more children with grammatical flexibility

The correlations with age of onset indicate that, on average, early-appearing verbs were used with grammatical flexibility by fewer children than later-appearing verbs. Such correlations might appear to be consistent with hypotheses that grammar emerges later, and thus perhaps as a consequence, of lexical development (e.g., Bates & Goodman, 1999). However, these correlations were only significant in the by-verb analysis; across children, the age at which children began to use verbs was unrelated to their composite grammatical flexibility. Similarly, the analyses of individual growth patterns by period of development, described earlier in this chapter, indicated that some of the children used their very first verbs with grammatical flexibility. This appears to be a case in which averaged data (in this case average properties of verbs rather than of individuals) present a picture that is true for some individuals but not for others (see Molenaar, 2008, for discussion).

CONCLUSIONS

In this chapter, we looked at the grammatical flexibility of early verb use in more detail, asking whether the overall grammatical flexibility we observed might obscure a limited, very early period of less flexible verb use and whether the lack of average differences between light and heavy verbs might obscure a pathbreaker role played by some light verbs for some children. We found that a small number of children did manifest conservative before flexible verb use, but the majority of children demonstrated flexibility close to the beginning, if not at the beginning, of verb use. We also found that sometimes a light verb was the first to appear with a particular syntactic frame, but that sometimes heavy verbs appeared in syntactic frames before light verbs. These findings support the conclusion that early flexible verb use is widespread and not limited to a late stage of development or a particular kind of verb. These findings also pointed out that descriptions of average developmental paths do not necessarily reflect all individual developmental paths.

We also asked whether different aspects of early verb use were related. Direct comparisons of the degree and onset of grammatical, semantic, and pragmatic flexibility yielded little indication of differences between these domains; however, the correlations were more informative. Across children, grammatical flexibility and semantic flexibility of verb use were related to each other; similarly, verbs showing actor flexibility with more children also showed grammatical flexibility with more children. These findings are consistent with many hypotheses about the interrelation between lexical and grammatical development: The correlations may reflect the effect of a common underlying ability and/or common effects of input, and the correlations may also indicate mutually supportive effects of syntactic understandings on semantics and vice versa. The hypothesis that grammar emerges once the lexicon reaches a particular threshold size received only very weak support—in a marginally significant correlation between the number of the target verbs children used at 21 months and their overall grammatical flexibility of verb usage. Although we found that those verbs that appeared at younger ages were used with grammatical flexibility by fewer children, on average, than were those verbs acquired at later ages, we do not interpret this as reflecting a pregrammatical period of verb use because children who began verb use earlier were not less grammatically flexible in their verb uses than children who began later. We did find that those children who began to use verbs earlier showed greater semantic flexibility. Thus, earlier-learned verbs may be used with less grammatical flexibility, but earlier verb-learning children are likely to be more semantically flexible. We consider these findings again in the discussion of the theoretical implications of these data.

VII. GENERAL DISCUSSION

The topic of this monograph is children's first uses of their first verbs. In the past decade and a half, the study of verb development has burgeoned, including experimental investigations of early verb comprehension and verb learning, studies of production using samples of spontaneous speech, and a diary study of one child's early verb use (e.g., Fisher & Gleitman, 2002; Hirsh-Pasek & Golinkoff, 2006; Lieven, 2006; Tomasello, 1992; Tomasello & Merriman, 1995). There have not, however, been studies of several children in the very earliest stage of verb production that would provide a more generalizable description of early verb use than can a study of a single child. This absence of detailed documentation of the beginning of verb use was a significant gap in the data on verb development because there are disputes regarding the nature of early language representation and, indeed, the nature of the language acquisition process addressable by data on how children use their very first verbs. The present study was designed to fill this gap.

Starting before their children's production of any verbs, eight mothers kept records of their children's first 10 uses of 34 target verbs that the previous literature suggested should be among children's first verbs. For each instance of verb use, the mothers recorded the full utterance in which the verb appeared and also noted whether the utterance containing the verb served the function of a command or description, who or what was performing the verb action, and who or what was the object of the verb action. These diary records were coded to provide measures of the pragmatic, semantic, and grammatical flexibility of children's first verb uses. Our discussion of these data and of their theoretical implications is organized around the following questions:

1. To what extent are children's early verb uses *conservative* versus *flexible* in pragmatics and semantics?

2. To what extent are children's early verb uses *conservative* versus *flexible* in grammar?

3. To what extent is early flexibility particularly characteristic of only some (i.e., light, or pathbreaking) verbs?

4. To what extent are the flexibility of meaning and form related?

5. What are the theoretical implications of the observed pragmatic, semantic, and grammatical flexibility of children's first verb uses?

TO WHAT EXTENT ARE CHILDREN'S EARLY VERB USES CONSERVATIVE VERSUS FLEXIBLE IN PRAGMATICS AND SEMANTICS?

Pragmatic Flexibility

The data of this study suggest that children's early verb use is pragmatically flexible. All of the children produced at least some of their first verbs in both commands and descriptions, and the majority of the verbs were used as both commands and descriptions, by the same child (and these two functions captured >98% of the childrens recorded utterances). Thus, neither any child nor any verb appeared to be completely context bound in use and, by inference, in mental representation. There was, however, variation among verbs such that some verbs were used only in descriptive utterances, not commands; no verbs were used only in commands. The variation by verb can be attributed to differences in the verbs' inherent meanings and the suitability of these meanings for the command function (e.g., "Need" is not a sensible command). For all of the target verbs for which both commands and descriptions are plausible functions, children produced both commands and descriptions within the first 10 instances recorded. Furthermore, verbs used as commands were used with multiple addressees, suggesting that the children had representations of verb meaning that were sufficiently abstract to apply to multiple actors. Although we did not explicitly assess the situations in which children used their verbs, the fact that the verbs with the highest number of addressees were the ones with more general meanings (i.e., the light verbs *come*, *go*, *look*, *put*) suggests that the children were applying the verbs across situations. This flexibility of use across situations, combined with the verbs' use to multiple addressees, argues against an account of early verb use as context bound. This discovery of the flexibility of verb use across addressees and, probably, situations was possible only because of the diary method employed. Unlike the researcher recording a sample of conversation in a single setting, the mother keeping a diary observes children's verb uses in multiple settings with multiple conversational partners and potential addressees. Indeed, the addressees of the children's utterances included parents, siblings, other relatives, characters in television shows, and pets.

Semantic Flexibility

The data from this study also reveal semantic flexibility from the beginning of verb use, where semantic flexibility is defined as the use of a verb to refer to multiple appropriate actions enacted by different actors and on different affected objects within the first 10 instances of the child's production of that verb. (The actors and objects need not have been expressed in the utterance; the point is that the child's use indicates that his or her representation of the meaning of the verb is not restricted to something that a single actor does or something that is done to a single object.) Six of the eight children in this study used at least one of their verbs in reference to more than one action, and more than one third of the verbs produced (38%) were used to refer to multiple actions. A total of seven verbs (*come, cut, go, open, put, take, wash*) were produced in reference to multiple actions by at least half of the children.

All eight children in this study used at least some of their verbs with multiple actors within the first 10 uses of those verbs, and most of the target verbs produced by these children (73%) were used with multiple actors within the first 10 uses. Moreover, the children's very first use of approximately half of their verbs was in reference to an actor other than themselves. Where actor extendability was limited, the limitations seemed to reflect verb meaning rather than linguistic limitations within the child. Children have little access to others' wants, needs, and likes, so *want, need,* and *like* were used primarily in self-reference. Other restricted actor uses may reflect restricted occasions to use particular verbs (e.g., *roll* is used only when there is a ball and thus *ball* is the only actor to appear with *roll*) (Naigles & Hoff, 2006).

Affected object flexibility was even greater than actor flexibility: All children used at least some verbs in reference to actions with more than one affected object, and 90% of the transitive and alternating verbs were used to refer to an action on more than one affected object. There were more affected objects per verb in children's first 10 instances of use than there were actors per verb; the time elapsed between first verb use with a different affected object was less than the time between first verb use and first use with a new actor, and all children showed a higher degree of affected object flexibility than actor flexibility. Thus, most of the time, children did not restrict their talk about two-argument relations to a single patient or theme; instead, they used their verbs in relation to up to eight different patients or themes within 10 uses. These are the first findings in the early verb-learning literature to document such a high level of semantic flexibility in production. They are consistent with the evidence of early flexibility from studies of verb comprehension using unconventional or novel affected objects (e.g., Naigles & Hoff, 2006). It is possible that the asymmetry between actor and affected object flexibility reflects a difference in the underlying representations of the actor and affected object roles such that children are more reluctant to extend a verb to a new actor than to a new patient or theme. However, we think a practical explanation is more likely: In the child's world, there exists a wider variety of possible affected objects than actors. That is, actors in children's worlds are mostly animate beings and these consist of family and friends. In contrast, affected objects are primarily inanimate objects, and these include all kinds of food, toys, household items, and so on. The set of possible affected objects is just bigger than the set of possible actors.

Importantly, actor flexibility and affected object flexibility patterned together—they were combined in the composite measure of semantic flexibility in the analyses of the intercorrelations among verb use measures; their zero-order correlation was both positive and significant, $r(n = 8) = .831$, $p = .011$. The finding that children who demonstrated more and earlier affected object flexibility also demonstrated more and earlier actor flexibility suggests that there was no tradeoff in which cognitive resources allocated to one area resulted in fewer resources available for the other. Moreover, the children who were early verb learners overall were also the ones showing more semantic flexibility, indicating that semantic flexibility is not a property of verb learning at a later developmental stage.

The present finding of actor flexibility in children's first verb uses is at odds with Huttenlocher et al.'s (1983) report that toddlers preferred to use verbs in reference to themselves; however, the discrepancy is explicable in terms of the difference in methods used. Huttenlocher et al. sampled dyadic mother–child interaction in a single setting, and thus only two possible actors were available. The diary method, in contrast, was able to tap uses across the day and across different settings in which other participants may be available. The fact that many instances of actor flexibility in our data set involved siblings or pets, who are not usually included in recording sessions, adds further credence to this methodological explanation. In fact, each child demonstrated actor flexibility with at least one verb by describing the action of his/her pet. Furthermore, the present findings of actor flexibility are consistent with the findings of comprehension studies, which show that toddlers can extend familiar and newly taught verbs to new actors and/or agents (Naigles & Hoff, 2006; Naigles et al., 2005; Poulin-Dubois & Forbes, 2006).

However, the children's extension of new verbs to new actors was not instantaneous. On average, children had a verb in their lexicon for half a month and used it three times before extending it to a new actor. Thus, it is still possible that Poulin-Dubois and Forbes's (2006) finding (see also Maguire et al., 2006) that 20-month-olds do not consistently match just-learned verbs to their actions when these are performed by new actors may indeed reflect an initial reluctance children have (within the 10 minutes usually provided) to extend a novel verb's action to a new actor. And perhaps the contrast between Naigles et al.'s (2005) findings that children do extend verb meanings and other researchers' findings that they do not suggests that presenting the verbs with different actors, as Naigles et al. did during training, helps children make their own extensions. In the real world, most children would experience most common verbs with multiple actors well before the onset of speech; therefore, it seems that if such experience is the crucial factor for actor extendability then most children would have had this experience and be able to generalize to new actions presented with only one actor. So why were the 1-year-olds in the present study more flexible in production than others have demonstrated in comprehension? A likely possibility is that 1-year-olds are simply less efficient learners, such that (in the absence of experiencing multiple actors) they need more time with the teaching stimulus (more than the 18 or so seconds usually provided in experimental settings), or possibly more time after teaching, to consolidate the representation before extending the verb to an action performed by a novel actor. Context-bound use, then, may be more a function of the amount of experience or time with particular verbs rather than a property of the overall course of verb learning.

These findings also cast doubt on Golinkoff et al.'s (1995) proposal that the principle of extendability that children apply to new nouns must be relearned for verbs. The speed with which our eight children demonstrated action, actor, and affected object flexibility (within 10 to 16 days of the first use of that verb) suggests that whatever principle was acquired for noun learning was easily and rapidly transferred to use with verbs. Stated in more general terms, the picture of early flexible verb use suggested by the present data contrasts with those descriptions in the literature that paint early word use, in general, as context bound. While instances of underextension are attested, underextended usage may be more characteristic of nouns, whose acquisition begins earlier in English, than of verbs. Our data show that early verb use is not typically context bound.

TO WHAT EXTENT ARE CHILDREN'S EARLY VERB USES CONSERVATIVE VERSUS FLEXIBLE IN GRAMMAR?

The data from this study show clearly that within their first 10 instances of producing a verb in spontaneous speech, children demonstrate flexibility in the syntactic environments in which those verbs appear. The children used multiple frames with two thirds of their verbs, and these first verbs were used in different frames, on average, by two thirds of the children. On average, children's first change in syntactic frame took place within half a month of the first verb use; thus, there was no extended period of frozen form use. On average, only 12% of such frame changes included the use of negation (range 0–36% across children; on average, 1.8% of utterances included negation markers); therefore, most of the frame flexibility observed involved children's flexibility in the argument structure of the verb. Morphological flexibility, reflecting just the children's uses of verbal suffixes, occurred at a much lower rate. Some children did not use any inflections with their verbs (most of the morphological forms that were used were "-ing") and examples of past tense or third-person singular use were rare. Changes—the addition or subtraction of such a morpheme—took close to a month to be observed after the first use.

Another measure of flexibility in verb use was the extent to which verbs were used with different lexical items in the preposition slot or in the subject or object positions. Children demonstrated flexibility in filling all these grammatical slots with multiple lexical items. In particular, the children showed lexical subject flexibility, in which a verb was used with at least two different subjects, with approximately one third of their verbs; just over one third of the children used verbs with multiple subjects. Lexical object flexibility was demonstrated by verbs for just under half of the children and by children for just under half of their verbs. Preposition flexibility was seen in five of the six children who produced prepositions at all. Tellingly, these indicators of lexical flexibility cohered with the other measures of grammatical flexibility in forming a composite grammatical flexibility score.

Finally, our analyses of individual differences in syntactic flexibility (Figures 10–18) investigated the developmental course of syntactic flexibility in each child. Contrary to the conservative-child hypothesis, fewer than half of our children ($n = 3$) demonstrated initial conservative verb-only use followed by later syntactic flexibility (i.e., after using verbs for 4–5 months). More tellingly, five children demonstrated use of verbs with arguments from the start of verb acquisition; for two of these children, syntactic flexibility with multiple verbs was evident within the first 6 weeks of verb use. For the others, syntactic flexibility in the use of one verb appeared during the first period and more verbs came to be used with flexibility during the subsequent 8 weeks—and almost always before the age of 2 years.

In addition to these measures of grammatical flexibility, we also applied to the present data corpus-based measures of productivity that have been employed in the literature (Ingram, 1989; Shirai, 1998). We found that using the more stringent criterion—that a frame must be used with five different verbs to be considered productive—the number of productive frames children had at 24 months was positively correlated with the overall measure of grammatical flexibility of their verb use. This correlation is consistent with the argument that flexibility is an indicator of productivity. We found that many of the children who achieved 3-Verb or 5-Verb productivity with a given frame (e.g., using VO with three or five different verbs) did so before the age of 24 months; three children even achieved such productivity with almost all of the relevant frames before 24 months of age. Across the entire corpus of first uses of first verbs, we found that the children used the SV and VO frames with >60% of their target verbs, the SVO frame with almost half of their target verbs, and the VP and V-ing frames with fewer, but still multiple verbs. Thus, well before 36 months of age—and frequently even before 24 months of age—the children provided evidence that their frames were not necessarily restricted to specific lexical items.

The measures of productivity and flexibility employed in the present study are only indirect measures of hallmark productivity, as we were unable to assess how any of the children's utterances diverged from their input. Indeed, the children had likely heard these verbs used flexibly by the adults around them. The picture of early verb use that these measures reveal, however, is in stark contrast to the description of early verb use that has been the basis for claims that young children are *not* productive verb users. With a variety of different measures, some assessing children's verb use across frames and others assessing children's frame use across verbs, these eight children have demonstrated that their early verb use was flexible rather than restricted and thus more consistent with an account of children's early verb use as reflecting abstract underlying knowledge than with a description of early verb use as strict imitations of input. The abstract knowledge need not be innate, as the traditional generativist position would hold. Rather, children's flexible verb usage may reflect children's learning that flexibility is general characteristic of verb use from the evidence of flexible uses of particular verbs in their input. Put another way, children's flexible verb uses may reflect learning from input, but it is learning that is more abstract than learning the multiple uses of individual verbs modeled in the input.

TO WHAT EXTENT IS EARLY FLEXIBILITY PARTICULARLY CHARACTERISTIC OF ONLY SOME (i.e., LIGHT, OR PATHBREAKING) VERBS?

The picture of early grammatical flexibility of verb use suggested by the present data was not limited to only some verbs. There was no evidence of a special pathbreaking role for light verbs in early grammatical development. Light verbs were neither the earliest verbs produced, nor were they, as a class, the verbs with the earliest or greatest syntactic or morphological flexibility. Of the 11 verbs produced before the age of 620 days (on average), some were light (*come, go*) but others were not (*throw, sit, see, push, open, lay, fall, eat, bite*). Moreover, when the children are considered individually, only

97

one child consistently demonstrated an advantage for light verbs, such that her first use of each frame and first instances of grammatical flexibility were shown for light verbs. Only sporadic evidence of a light verb advantage was found for three other children, and for the other four children none of their light verbs showed more grammatical flexibility than heavy verbs that emerged at the same age. When the frames were considered individually, only the SVO frame consistently appeared first with a single verb, and this verb (*want* for six of the eight children) was hardly the most semantically transparent. For all other frames, the verbs that appeared first varied widely across children and were neither consistently semantically transparent nor consistently highly frequent in the input. Taken together, then, our findings do not support the proposals (e.g., Chenu & Jisa, 2006; Goldberg, 1999; Ninio, 1999) that light verbs are the primary promoters of grammatical development.

There were, however, several indications in our data that the children did use light verbs differently than heavy verbs. Light verbs appeared more frequently in commands and less frequently in descriptions than did heavy verbs. Moreover, light verbs were used with multiple addressees more than heavy verbs; they were also used with more different affected objects than heavy verbs, and there was a trend in the same direction for a greater use of different actors with light than with heavy verbs. Finally, light verbs appeared with direct objects and in SVO frames more frequently than heavy verbs did, and they were used with more and earlier lexical object flexibility than heavy verbs. All of these findings derive in a straightforward fashion from differences in the meanings of light and heavy verbs. The association of light verbs with commands can be attributed to the behavior of three verbs in particular, *come*, *go*, and *look*, which seem likely to be commonly used as commands in input as well. In contrast, the heavy subclass included more verbs referring to internal states (*like*, *need*, *cry*), which could not be used as commands. Furthermore, the more general verbs in the light verb subclass can apply to more different situations and so can be used with more different actors, affected objects, and addressees. That is, anyone can *go* or *come* and anything can be *brought* or *taken*, whereas only eatables can be *eaten* and only animates can *eat*. And because heavy verbs refer directly and obviously to specific events in the world, their direct objects can be omitted because of common ground between speaker and hearer whereas these forms need to be retained with more general verbs. The children seemed aware, at some level, of the need of the addressee to have some affected objects made more explicit than others (see also Matthews et al., 2006). If such objects are required more with light verbs by the dictates of common ground, then, because of base rates, more different NPs should be used. Thus, the grammatical advantage of light verbs, appearing more with objects and in SVO frames, is directly traceable to the semantic/

pragmatic requirements of those verbs in usage, not to their unique mapping onto the semantics of specific frames. This is consistent with Snedeker and Gleitman's (2004) suggestion that light verbs, because of their applicability to such a wide variety of situations, must be the products rather than the engines of early grammatical acquisition.

TO WHAT EXTENT ARE THE FLEXIBILITY OF MEANING AND OF FORM RELATED?

Semantic flexibility and grammatical flexibility of verb use were related, both as properties of children and as properties of verbs. The children who showed more semantic flexibility in their first verb uses (indexed by a composite of multiple measures) also showed more grammatical flexibility (also indexed by a composite score). Among the target verbs in this study, those that were used with grammatical flexibility by more children were also used with multiple actors by more children. Thus, these findings extend theoretical accounts of the relations between early verb syntax and verb semantics in a couple of ways. The findings suggest that it is not just knowing a certain number of verbs (Marchman & Bates, 1994) but also having the understandings that underlie semantic flexibility of verb use that supports the acquisition of verb grammar (Naigles et al., 2005). The findings also suggest that the relationship between semantic flexibility and syntactic flexibility is reciprocal. In particular, the finding that semantic flexibility and syntactic flexibility were related as properties of verbs, in addition to being related as properties of children, supports the syntactic bootstrapping hypothesis: Verbs used with more grammatical flexibility are verbs with more elaborate semantic representations as well.

The semantic and grammatical flexibility of verb use did, however, differ in their relations to the age at which the child began to use verbs and to when the verb appeared in the children's speech. Children who began verb use at a younger age showed, on average, greater semantic flexibility in their verb use. Children may become early verb learners, then, if they have early acquired the ability to extract verb referents from their observed contexts. In contrast, these earlier verb learners did not show greater—or lesser—grammatical flexibility in their early verb uses, nor did they achieve a greater—or lesser—number of productive frames by the age of 24 months compared with children who began to use verbs later. Earlier verb learners, then, may be specifically precocious in their ability to extend their verb *meanings* in multiple ways, but they are neither advanced nor behind other children in their ability to use those verbs in multiple ways in terms of *grammar*. Among verbs, however, the picture is a bit different: Those verbs that appeared earlier in the children's speech were used with grammatical flexibility (in their first 10 uses) by fewer children than were later-appearing verbs, but age of appearance showed no relation to the proportion of children who used a verb with semantic flexibility. Thus, the data present a picture in which children who begin to use verbs earlier use their first verbs with a similar degree of grammatical flexibility as children who begin later, but verbs that are used earlier than other verbs are used with grammatical flexibility by fewer children. Less grammatical flexibility, then, is a property of earlier-learned verbs but not of earlier-verb-learning children. It is important to point out, though, even the earliest-learned verb (*open*) was used with grammatical flexibility by almost 30% of the children. Overall, we found no evidence that there exist early-learned verbs, or early-starting children, that are *consistently* inflexible.

THEORETICAL IMPLICATIONS OF THE OBSERVED PRAGMATIC, SEMANTIC, AND GRAMMATICAL FLEXIBILITY OF CHILDREN'S FIRST VERB USES

The data from this diary study indicate that 1-year-old children use their newly acquired verbs flexibly, in multiple situations, with multiple actions, actors, affected objects, and paths or locations. These findings are at odds with models of acquisition in which children's verb meanings are initially conservative (e.g., Golinkoff et al., 1995; Maguire et al., 2006). The present data show that 1-year-old children also use their verbs in different sentence frames, with different subjects, objects, and prepositions, and (somewhat) with different morphology, all within the first 10 instances of use. Such flexible use suggests as well that children younger than 2 years do not, in fact, manifest the restricted use that inspired the Verb Island Hypothesis. These findings are more consistent with the generativist view of child language acquisition (e.g., Chomsky, 1981; Gleitman & Fisher, 2002) than with the positions that children are conservative language users and that 2-year-olds do not have abstract syntax (e.g., Goldberg, 1999; Lieven, 2006; Tomasello, 2000).

However, in the present data, fully flexible and productive verb use was not evident in all children from the moment verb use began. On average, the percent of verbs that children used flexibly varied from 16% (morphology) to 30% (lexical subjects) to 38% (actions) to 46% (lexical objects) to 50% (addressees) to 66% (syntax) to 73% (actors) to 90% (affected objects). Every child produced *some* verbs in the same way (i.e., conservatively) on the pragmatic, lexical, and/or grammatical measures for all of their first 10 instances. Even when verb uses were flexible across the first 10 instances, they were rarely flexible by the second instance. Thus, children were swift to show some kinds of flexibility and productivity but did not demonstrate all kinds of flexibility and productivity instantaneously. Moreover, some children appeared to be swifter and/or more flexible and productive than others.

There are two possible, and not mutually exclusive, sources of this variability in the flexibility with which children use their first verbs. A generativist would argue that the children had full grammatical knowledge from the beginning but that a variety of personality, pragmatic, and contextual factors limited children's expression of that underlying grammatical knowledge. That is, some children are more interested than others in talking about new things, and to new people, than other children (Nelson, 1973; Reznick, Corley, & Robinson, 1997); some verbs afford more flexible use than others and sometimes the occasions for the use of a verb may be limited. Consistent with this position, comprehension studies, where such pragmatic-, semantic-, and personality-based influences should not apply, indicate that most toddlers demonstrate significant generalization of most newly introduced lexical items (e.g., Gertner et al., 2006; Naigles et al., 2005; Poulin-Dubois & Forbes, 2006). Future comprehension investigations could further solidify these findings by extending the semantic and grammatical properties studied (e.g., to novel affected objects, and to [in the relevant languages] PPs and case markers).

Also consistent with the present data, though, is a model in which grammatical knowledge is not fully present from the beginning. Some grammatical understandings are achieved before any verb use in production resulting in the flexibility that is observed, but some grammatical understandings develop after production begins. The clear frame differences and individual differences in these data suggest that the correct description of children as verb learners will contain elements of both the rapid generalizer and conservative-child accounts, in different measure for different children, different verbs, and different frames (see Maratsos, 2007, for a similar argument in a different domain). When all the supportive factors are in place (e.g., the verbs have been used flexibly in the input, the child is feeling talkative, the situation is new and interesting but not too new and interesting, and possibly the frame is more transparent), children are more likely to be swiftly flexible and productive—and possibly even show generalization to novel instances, although such latter demonstrations are unlikely to be manifest in spontaneous speech. When the supportive factors are not in place, children may be more likely to be conservative, and some supportive factors may be more available for some verbs than for others. Differences among children in their speech processing abilities may also lead to variation in the onset or rate of flexibility, productivity, and generalization, consonant with other recent findings that early perceptual factors predict later language measures (Fernald, Perfors, & Marchman, 2006; Kuhl, Conboy, Padden, Nelson, & Pruitt, 2005; Newman, Bernstein Ratner, Jusczyk, Jusczyk, & Dow, 2006).

Thus, one position consistent with our data is that abstract grammatical categories are learned from input, but the process of learning begins early, before speech production at all or before production of the relevant linguistic frame or construction. As summarized by Gerken (2007; see also Naigles, 2002; Saffran & Thiessen, 2007), researchers have demonstrated that considerable knowledge about the patterns—at varying levels of abstractness—of a given language are accrued during the first 12–18 months of life. If children have indeed been actively processing their input language for over a year by the time they produce their first verbs, then perhaps it is not surprising that they should show the level of productivity and flexibility that our data reveal (see also Snyder, 2007, for a concurring view from a more generativist framework). Similarly, if grammatical development awaits the achievement of a threshold of lexical development, it is a threshold that children achieve very early.

The present findings have some further implications for accounts of the process or processes that underlie language development. The observed intercorrelations between the grammatical flexibility and semantic flexibility of verb use (Tables 25 and 26, chapter VI) suggest there may be some common learning processes and/or common experiences that support both semantic and grammatical development. The correlations by verb, in particular, suggest that syntactic properties of verbs reveal their semantic possibilities, and vice versa. For example, learning quickly that *open* can be used with multiple affected objects might enable children to quickly understand that it should also appear with grammatical objects; learning quickly that *run* does not involve affected objects effectively limits its grammatical uses and distinguishes them from those of *open*. Another way to think about this is that whatever input enables verbs' semantics to be learned quickly also enables their grammatical aspects—the information relevant for meaning is also relevant for grammar. The input interpretation is consistent with the findings of Naigles and Hoff-Ginsberg (1998), who found that verbs used with more syntactic diversity by mothers are the ones used more frequently and with more syntactic diversity by children 10 weeks later.

The present findings suggest that the relevant question for future research, then, is not *whether* children—toddlers, even—can be flexible and productive with syntactic frames and extend lexical semantic meanings. Clearly, they can. The issue is really, *how early in development*, and *how quickly upon meeting a new verb*, do they do this and what factors influence this process.

LIMITATIONS

This study is, of course, limited by the fact that we have investigated the development of only a small number (34) of verbs and have tracked their development for only their first 10 uses. In particular, our exclusion of *make* and *do* from the targeted verbs limits our conclusions about the grammatical contributions of light verbs, as these have been proposed as the pathbreakers for the transitive frame (Goldberg, 1999; Ninio, 1999). However, our verbs were chosen because previous data indicated that these 34 were among the earliest produced by 1-year-old English learners (e.g., Naigles & Hoff-Ginsberg, 1998); therefore, we do not anticipate that many other verbs would elicit earlier use and/or flexibility. Moreover, when the first uses of *make* were examined for two of the children, whose mothers recorded them at their own initiative (Mae and Stacey; see Tables 20 and 23, respectively), there was no evidence that *make* functioned as a pathbreaker for either one.

The generalizability of the present findings is also limited by the fact that we have only included eight children, although an *n* of 8 is large for the individual data analytic approach employed in this study. Because the current method excluded, for different reasons, both children who were extremely talkative and those who talked very little (see chapter II), the range of behavior of American English-learning toddlers at large is probably wider than seen here. It is likely that both more and less swiftly flexible children exist. Our conclusions might also be limited by the fact that we relied on the parents to note each of the first 10 instances of these 34 verbs, including self-repetitions. However, we have reason to believe that these eight mothers carried out just this task. First, we talked to each parent every week, once their child had begun producing verbs, giving them weekly reminders of how to report the relevant aspects of their children's verb use to the diary pages. Mothers who were not able to do this were quite open to telling us. Only the children whose mothers were able to carry out the task in the manner prescribed are included in the study. Moreover, if our documented child variations reflected only maternal variation in keeping the diary, then children should differ, consistently, in how speedy or slow they were to reach 10 instances, or in how flexible they were on all measures. That is, if some mothers were consistently more conscientious or more attuned to their child's speech, then some children should show precocity on all measures whereas other children should be consistently slow. In contrast, though, all of our children produced all 10 instances of at least some verbs in a very short period of time and all also took a very long time to reach 10 instances of other verbs (chapter III).

Finally, it is possible that, because they were listening for their children's use of these verbs, the mothers might have been more likely to use those verbs, themselves. More frequent use by mothers, though, would only have led to earlier use by the children, not to more or less flexible or productive use. That is, there is no reason to expect that more frequent use by mothers would have also meant more diverse use by mothers—in fact, we would argue that the folk theories of language "training" held by most middle-class mothers would lead them to less diverse uses (i.e., repetitions of the same verb phrases). Thus, it seems quite unlikely that the mothers' keeping of diary records altered the development under study.

CONCLUSIONS

The overall picture of the functions, meanings, and grammar of verbs when they first appear in children's speech is one of flexible use. Children use their verbs in utterances that serve multiple communicative functions, with multiple actors and affected objects, and in multiple syntactic frames. This picture contrasts with descriptions in the literature of early verb use as restricted and context bound. Part of the explanation for these differing descriptions of early verb use may be in the unique nature of the database for the present analyses. Our database provided the completeness of sampling that is characteristic of diary studies, but our database included several children. Thus, our data reveal that whereas individual children can have restricted uses of individual verbs, restricted use is not a stage of language development through which all children pass. Like children's overextensions (e.g., calling strange men *Daddy*; Rescorla, 1980) and over regularizations (e.g., *goed*) (Marcus, Pinker, Ullman, Hollander, Rosen, & Xu, 1992), instances of context-bound and grammatically restricted verb use may be more salient than they are frequent.

The present findings argue that children are not as conservative language learners as some theories of language acquisition would have them be, either in meaning or in structure. At least for verb learning, they do not start small, with verb-specific grammars, but instead begin in the middle, with some flexibility and productivity manifested by the time they begin to use verbs at all. Children quickly match their input, observing from the very beginning of language use the subcategorization distinctions in the target language. Within their first 10 uses of newly acquired verbs children show that their grammars include *categories* of verbs, which are differentiated by grammatical privileges of occurrence. They do not appear to have a single category, *VERB*, in which all verbs are treated equally, nor do they seem to have 34 separate and isolated verb-specific representations. To reveal these findings, we had to develop a new method—a diary that targeted only verbs and that asked mothers to record only their child's first 10 instances of use. By restricting the aspects of language use, we made the diary tractable for data collectors such that more children could be studied. By using the diary method, we were able to collect uses in almost all of the contexts in which children talk. And by asking for 10 successive instances, we were able to demonstrate that—and track how—children's very first uses changed.

REFERENCES

Akhtar, N., & Tomasello, M. (1997). Young children's productivity with word order and verb morphology. *Developmental Psychology*, **33**, 952–965.

Akhtar, N., & Tomasello, M. (2000). The social nature of words and word learning. In R. Golinkoff, K. Hirsh-Pasek, & L. Bloom (Eds.), *Becoming a word learner: A debate on lexical acquisition* (pp. 115–135). New York: Oxford University Press.

Allen, S. E. M., & Schroder, H. (2003). Preferred argument structure in early Inuktitut spontaneous speech data. In J. W. DuBois, L. E. Kumpf, & W. J. Ashby (Eds.), *Preferred argument structure: Grammar as architecture for function* (pp. 301–338). Amsterdam: John Benjamins.

Ambridge, B., Theakston, A. L., Lieven, E. V. M., & Tomasello, M. (2006). The distributed learning effect for children's acquisition of an abstract syntactic construction. *Cognitive Development*, **21**, 174–193.

Armon-Lotem, S., & Berman, R. A. (2003). The emergence of grammar: Early verbs and beyond. *Journal of Child Language*, **30**, 845–877.

Baldwin, D. A. (1993). Infant's ability to consult the speaker for clues to word reference. *Journal of Child Language*, **20**, 395–418.

Barrett, M., Harris, M., & Chasin, J. (1991). Early lexical development and maternal speech: A comparison of children's initial and subsequent uses of words. *Journal of Child Language*, **18**, 21–40.

Bates, E., Bretherton, I., & Snyder, L. (1988). *From first words to grammar: Individual differences and dissociable mechanisms*. New York: Cambridge University Press.

Bates, E., & Goodman, J. (1999). On the emergence of grammar from the lexicon. In B. MacWhinney (Ed.), *The emergence of language* (pp. 29–80). New Jersey: Erlbaum.

Bloom, L. (1973). *One word at a time: The use of single word utterances*. The Hague: Mouton.

Bloom, L. (1993). *Language development from two to three*. Cambridge, UK: Cambridge University Press.

Bloom, L., Lifter, K., & Hafitz, J. (1980). Semantics of verbs and the development of verb inflection in child language. *Language*, **56**, 386–412.

Borer, H., & Wexler, K. (1987). The maturation of syntax. In T. Roeper & E. Williams (Eds.), *Parameter setting* (pp. 123–187). Dordrecht: Reidel.

Bowerman, M. (1973). Structural relationships in children's utterances: Syntactic or semantic? In T. E. Moore (Ed.), *Cognitive development and the acquisition of language* (pp. 197–214). New York: Academic Press.

Braunwald, S. (1995). Differences in the acquisition of early verbs: Evidence from diary data from sisters. In M. Tomasello & W. Merriman (Eds.), *Beyond names for things: Young children's acquisition of verbs* (pp. 81–111). Hillsdale, NJ: Erlbaum.

Brent, M. R. (1993). From grammar to lexicon: Unsupervised learning of lexical syntax. *Computational Linguistics*, **19**, 243–262.

Campbell, A., & Tomasello, M. (2001). The acquisition of dative constructions. *Applied Psycholinguistics*, **22**, 253–267.

Caselli, M. C., Casadio, P., & Bates, E. (1999). A comparison of the transition from first words to grammar in English and Italian. *Journal of Child Language*, **26**, 69–111.

Casenhiser, D., & Goldberg, A. E. (2005). Fast mapping between a phrasal form and meaning. *Developmental Science*, **8**, 500–508.

Chenu, F., & Jisa, H. (2006). Caused motion constructions and semantic generality in early acquisition of French. In E. Clark & B. Kelly (Eds.), *Constructions in acquisition* (pp. 233–261). Stanford, CA: CSLI Publications.

Childers, J., & Tomasello, M. (2006). Are nouns easier to acquire than verbs? In K. Hirsch-Pasek & R. Golinkoff (Eds.), *Action meets word: How children learn verbs* (pp. 311–335). New York: Oxford University Press.

Chomsky, N. (1975). *Reflections on language*. New York:Pantheon Books.

Chomsky, N. (1981). *Lectures on government and binding*. Holland: Foris Publications.

Clark, E. V. (1987). The principle of contrast: A constraint on language acquisition. In B. MacWhinney (Ed.), *Mechanisms of language acquisition* (pp. 1–33). Hillsdale, NJ: Erlbaum.

Clark, E. V. (1993). *The lexicon in acquisition*. Cambridge, UK: Cambridge University Press.

Clark, E. V. (2003). *First language acquisition*. Cambridge, UK: Cambridge University Press.

Clark, H. (1996). *Using language*. Cambridge, UK: Cambridge University Press.

Clark, H. H. (1973). The language-as-fixed-effect fallacy: A critique of language statistics in psychological research. *Journal of Verbal Learning and Verbal Behavior*, **12**, 335–359.

Conboy, B. T., & Thal, D. J. (2006). Ties between the lexicon and grammer: Cross-sectional and longitudinal studies of bilingual toddlers. *Child development*, **77**, 712–735.

Crain, S., & Lillo-Martin, D. (1999). *An introduction to linguistic theory and language acquisition*. Oxford, UK: Blackwell Publishers.

Demuth, K. (1996). Collecting spontaneous production data. In D. McDaniel, C. McKee & H. S. Cairns (Eds.), *Methods for assessing children's syntax* (pp. 3–22). Cambridge, MA: MIT Press.

Dixon, J., & Marchman, V. A. (2007). Grammar and the lexicon: Developmental ordering in language acquisition. *Child Development*, **78**, 190–212.

Dromi, E. (1987). *Early lexical development*. Cambridge, UK: Cambridge University Press.

Elman, J. L., Bates, E. A., Johson, M. H., Karmiloff-Smith, A., Parisi, D., & Plunkett, K. (1996). *Rethinking innateness: A connectionist perspective on development*. Cambridge, MA: MIT Press.

Fenson, L., Dale, P., Reznick, J., Bates, E., Thal, D., & Pethick, S. (1994). Variability in early communicative development. *Monographs of the Society for Research in Child Development*, **59**(5, Serial No. 242).

Fernald, A., Perfors, A., & Marchman, V. (2006). Picking up speed in understanding: Speech processing efficiency and vocabulary growth across the second year. *Developmental Psychology*, **42**, 98–116.

Fernandes, K. J., Marcus, G. F., Di Nubila, J. A., & Vouloumanos, A. (2006). From semantics to syntax and back again: Argument structure in the third year of life. *Cognition*, **100**, B10–B20.

Fisher, C. (1996). Structural limits on verb mapping: The role of analogy in children's interpretations of sentences. *Cognitive Psychology*, **31**, 41–81.

Fisher, C., Gleitman, H., & Gleitman, L. (1991). On the semantic content of subcategorization frames. *Cognitive Psychology*, **23**, 331–392.

Fisher, C., & Gleitman, L. R. (2002). Language acquisition. In H. Pashler (Series Ed.) & Gallistel, R. (Vol. Ed.), *Steven's handbook of experimental psychology: Vol. 3. Learning, motivation, and emotion* (3rd ed., pp. 445–496). Hoboken, NJ: John Wiley & Sons.

Forbes, J. N., & Poulin-Dubois, D. (1997). Representational change in young children's understanding of familiar verb meaning. *Journal of Child Language*, **24**, 389–406.

Gentner, D., & Boroditsky, L. (2002). Individuation, relativity, and early word learning. In M. Bowerman & S. Levinson (Eds.), *Language acquisition and conceptual development* (pp. 215–256). Cambridge, UK: Cambridge University Press.

Gerken, L. (2007). Acquiring linguistic structure. In E. Hoff & M. Shatz (Eds.), *Blackwell handbook of language development* (pp. 173–190). Oxford, UK: Blackwell Publishing.

Gertner, Y., Fisher, C., & Eisengart, J. (2006). Learning words and rules: Abstract knowledge of word order in early sentence comprehension. *Psychological Science*, **17**, 684–691.

Gillette, J., Gleitman, H., Gleitman, L., & Lederer, A. (1999). Human simulations of vocabulary learning. *Cognition*, **73**, 135–176.

Gleitman, L. (1990). The structural sources of verb meanings. *Language Acquisition*, **1**, 3–55.

Gleitman, L. R., & Newport, E. L. (1995). The invention of language by children: Environmental and biological influences on the acquisition of language. In L. R. Gleitman & M. Liberman (Eds.), *An invitation to cognitive science: Vol. 1. Language* (2nd ed., pp. 1–24). Cambridge, MA: MIT Press.

Goldberg, A. (1999). The emergence of the semantics of argument structure constructions. In B. MacWhinney (Ed.), *The emergence of language* (pp. 197–211). Mahwah, NJ: Erlbaum.

Goldberg, A., & Casenhiser, D. (2006). Learning argument structure constructions. In E. Clark & B. Kelly (Eds.), *Constructions in acquisition* (pp. 185–204). Stanford, CA: CSLI Publications.

Goldberg, A. E., Casenhiser, D. M., & Sethuraman, N. (2004). Learning argument structure generalizations. *Cognitive Linguistics*, **15**, 289–316.

Goldin-Meadow, S. (2003). *The resilience of language: What gesture creation in deaf children can tell us about how all children learn language.* New York: Psychology Press.

Goldin-Meadow, S., Seligman, M. E., & Gelman, R. (1976). Language in the two-year-old. *Cognition*, **4**, 189–202.

Golinkoff, R., Hirsh-Pasek, K., Cauley, K., & Gordon, L. (1987). The eyes have it: Lexical and syntactic comprehension in a new paradigm. *Journal of Child Language*, **14**, 23–45.

Golinkoff, R. M., Hirsh-Pasek, K., Mervis, C. B., Frawley, W., & Parillo, M. (1995). Lexical principles can be extended to the acquisition of verbs. In M. Tomasello & W. Merriman (Eds.), *Beyond names for things: Young children's acquisition of verbs* (pp. 185–222). Hillsdale, NJ: Lawrence Erlbaum Associates.

Gómez, R. L. (2002). Variability and detection of invariant structure. *Psychological Science*, **13**, 431–436.

Goodman, J. C., McDonough, L., & Brown, N. B. (1998). The role of semantic context and memory in the acquisition of novel nouns. *Child Development*, **69**, 1330–1344.

Goodman, J. C., & Sethuraman, N. (2006). Interactions in the development of constructions and the acquisition of word meanings. In E. Clark & B. Kelly (Eds.), *Constructions in acquisition* (pp. 263–281). Stanford: CSLI Publications.

Grice, H. P. (Ed.) (1989). Further notes on logic and conversation. *Studies in the way of words* (pp. 41–57). Cambridge, MA: Harvard University Press. (Reprinted from *Syntax and semantics: Vol. 9. Pragmatics*, pp. 113–128, by P. Cole, Ed., 1978, New York: Academic Press).

Harris, M., Barrett, M., Jones, D., & Brooks, S. (1988). Linguistic input and early word meaning. *Journal of Child Language*, **15**, 77–94.

Hirsh-Pasek, K. & Golinkoff, R. (Eds.), (2006). *Action meets word: How children learn verbs.* Oxford UK: Oxford University Press.

Hirsh-Pasek, K., Golinkoff, R. M., Hennon, E. A., & Maguire, M. J. (2004). Hybrid theories at the frontier of developmental psychology: The emergentist coalition model of word learning as a case in point. In G. Hall & S. Waxman (Eds.), *Weaving a lexicon* (pp. 173–204). Cambridge, MA: MIT Press.

Hirsh-Pasek, K., Golinkoff, R., & Naigles, L. (1996). Young children's use of syntactic frames to derive meaning. In K. Hirsh-Pasek & R. Golinkoff (Eds.), *The origins of grammar: Evidence from early language comprehension* (pp. 123–158). Cambridge, MA: MIT Press.

Hollich, G. J., Hirsh-Pasek, K., & Golinkoff, R. M. (2000). Breaking the language barrier: An emergentist coalition model for the origins of word learning. *Monographs of the Society for Research in Child Development, 65*(3, Serial No.262).

Hopper, P. J., & Thompson, S. A. (1980). Transitivity in grammar and discourse. *Language, 56,* 251–299.

Huttenlocher, J., Smiley, P., & Charney, R. (1983). The emergence of action categories in the child: Evidence from verb meaning. *Psychological Review, 90,* 72–93.

Ingram, D. (1981). Early patterns of grammatical development. In R. Stark (Ed.) *Language behavior in infancy and early childhood* (pp. 327–352). New York: Elsevier North-Holland.

Ingram, D. (1989). *First language acquisition.* Cambridge, UK: Cambridge University Press.

Jackendoff, R. (1983). *Semantics and cognition.* Cambridge, MA: MIT Press.

Jackendoff, R. (1990). *Semantic structures.* Cambridge, MA: MIT Press.

Jackendoff, R. (2004). *Foundations of language: Brain, meaning, grammar, evolution.* New York: Oxford University Press.

Jackson-Maldonado, D., Thal, D., Marchman, V., Bates, E., & Guitierrez-Clellen, V. (1993). Early lexical development in Spanish-speaking infants and toddlers. *Journal of Child Language, 20,* 523–549.

Kidd, E., Lieven, E., & Tomasello, M. (2006). Examining the role of lexical frequency in children's acquisition and processing of sentential complements. *Cognitive Development, 21,* 93–107.

Kuhl, P., Conboy, B., Padden, D., Nelson, T., & Pruitt, J. (2005). Early speech perception and later language development: Implications for the "critical period". *Language Learning and Development, 1,* 237–264.

Landau, B., & Gleitman, L. R. (1985). *Language and experience: Evidence from the blind child.* Cambridge, MA: Harvard University Press.

Levin, B. (1993). *English verb classes and alternations: A preliminary investigation.* Chicago: The University of Chicago Press.

Lieven, E. (2006). Producing multiword utterances. In E. Clark & B. Kelly (Eds.), *Constructions in acquisition* (pp. 83–110). Stanford, CA: CSLI Publications.

Lieven, E., Behrens, H., Speares, J., & Tomasello, M. (2003). Early syntactic creativity: A usage-based approach. *Journal of Child Language, 30,* 333–367.

MacWhinney, B. (2004). A multiple process solution to the logical problem of language acquisition. *Journal of Child Language, 31,* 883–914.

Maguire, M. J., Hirsh-Pasek, K., & Golinkoff, R. M. (2006). A unified theory of word learning: Putting verb acquisition in context. In K. Hirsh-Pasek & R. Golinkoff (Eds.), *Action meets word: How children learn verbs* (pp. 364–391). New York: Oxford University Press.

Maital, S., Dromi, E., Sagi, A., & Bornstein, M. H. (2000). The Hebrew communicative development inventory: Language specific properties and cross-linguistic generalizations. *Journal of Child Language, 27,* 43–67.

Maratsos, M. (2007). Commentary. *Monographs of the Society for Research in Child Development, 72,* 121–126.

Marchman, V., & Bates, E. (1994). Continuity in lexical and morphological development: A test of the critical mass hypothesis. *Journal of Child Language, 21,* 339–366.

Marchman, V. A., Martinez-Sussman, C., & Dale, P. S. (2004). The language-specific nature of grammatical development: Evidence from bilingual language learners. *Developmental Science, 7,* 212.

Marcus, G. F., Pinker, S., Ullman, M., Hollander, M., Rosen, T. J., & Xu, F. (1992). Overregularization in language acquisition. *Monographs of the society for Research in Child Development*, **57**(4, Serial No. 228).

Markman, E. (1989). *Categorization and naming in children: Problems of induction*. Cambridge, MA: MIT Press.

Matthews, D., Lieven, E., Theakston, A., & Tomasello, M. (2005). The role of frequency in the acquisition of English word order. *Cognitive Development*, **20**, 121–136.

Matthews, D., Lieven, E., Theakston, A., & Tomasello, M. (2006). The effect of perceptual availability and prior discourse on young children's use of referring expressions. *Applied Psycholinguistics*, **27**, 403–422.

McClure, K., Pine, J. M., & Lieven, E. V. M. (2006). Investigating the abstractness of children's early knowledge of argument structure. *Journal of Child Language*, **33**, 693–720.

McShane, J. (1980). *Learning to talk*. Cambridge, UK: Cambridge University Press.

Mervis, C. B. (1987). Child-basic object categories and early lexical development. In U. Neisser (Ed.), *Concepts and conceptual development: Ecological and intellectual factors in categorization* (pp. 201–233). New York: Cambridge University Press.

Mintz, T. (2003). Frequent frames as a cue for grammatical categories in child directed speech. *Cognition*, **90**, 91–117.

Molenaar, P. C. M. (2008). On the implications of the classical ergodic theorems: Analysis of developmental processes has to focus on intra-individual variation. *Developmental Psychobiology*, **50**, 60–69.

Naigles, L. (1990). Children use syntax to learn verb meanings. *Journal of Child Language*, **17**, 357–374.

Naigles, L. (1997). Are English-speaking one-year-olds verb learners, too? In E. Clark (Ed.), *Proceedings of the 28th annual child language research forum* (pp. 199–212). Stanford, CA: The Center for the Study of Language and Information.

Naigles, L. (1998). Developmental changes in the use of structure in verb learning. In C. Rovee-Collier, L. Lipsitt, & H. Hayne (Eds.), *Advances in infancy research* (Vol. 12, pp. 298–318). London: Ablex.

Naigles, L., Bavin, E., & Smith, M. (2005). Toddlers recognize verbs in novel situations and sentences. *Developmental Science*, **8**, 424–431.

Naigles, L., Gleitman, H., & Gleitman, L. R. (1993). Children acquire word meaning components from syntactic evidence. In E. Dromi (Ed.), *Language and cognition: A developmental perspective* (pp. 104–140). Norwood, NJ: Ablex.

Naigles, L., & Hoff-Ginsberg, E. (1995). Input to verb learning: Evidence for the plausibility of syntactic bootstrapping. *Developmental Psychology*, **31**, 827–837.

Naigles, L., & Hoff-Ginsberg, E. (1998). Why are some verbs learned before other verbs? Effects of input frequency and structure on children's early verb use. *Journal of Child Language*, **25**, 95–120.

Naigles, L. R. (2002). Form is easy, meaning is hard: Resolving a paradox in early child language. *Cognition*, **86**, 157–199.

Naigles, L. R. (2003). Paradox lost? No, paradox found! Reply to Tomasello & Akhtar (2003). *Cognition*, **88**, 325–329.

Naigles, L. R., & Hoff, E. (2006). Verbs at the very beginning: Parallels between comprehension and input. In K. Hirsh-Pasek & R. Golinkoff (Eds.), *Action meets word: How children learn verbs* (pp. 336–363). New York: Oxford University Press.

Naigles, L. R., & Swensen, L. D. (2007). Syntactic supports for word learning. In E. Hoff & M. Shatz (Eds.), *The handbook of language development* (pp. 212–231). New York: Blackwell.

Nelson, K. (1973). Structure and strategy in learning to talk. *Monographs of the Society for Research in Child Development*, **38**(1-2, Serial No. 149).

Newman, R., Bernstein Ratner, N., Jusczyk, A. M., Jusczyk, P. W., & Dow, K. A. (2006). Infants' early ability to segment the conversational speech signal predicts later language development: A retrospective analysis. *Developmental Psychology*, **42**, 643–655.

Ninio, A. (1999). Pathbreaking verbs in syntactic development and the question of proto-typical transitivity. *Journal of Child Language*, **26**, 619–653.

Ninio, A. (2005a). Testing the role of semantic similarity in syntactic development. *Journal of Child Language*, **32**, 35–61.

Ninio, A. (2005b). Accelerated learning without semantic similarity: Indirect objects. *Cognitive Linguistics*, **16**, 531–556.

Ninio, A. (2007). *Language and the learning curve: A new theory of syntactic development*. New York: Oxford University Press.

Ogura, T., Yamashita, Y., Murase, T., & Dale, P. S. (1993). Some findings from the Japanese early communicative development inventories. *Memoirs of the Faculty of Education, Shimane University*, **27**, 26–38. (In English).

Olguin, R., & Tomasello, M. (1993). Twenty-five month old children do not have a grammatical category of verb. *Cognitive Development*, **8**, 245–272.

Pine, J., Lieven, E., & Rowland, C. (1998). Comparing different models of the development of the English verb category. *Linguistics*, **36**, 807–830.

Pinker, S. (1984). *Language learnability and language development*. Cambridge, MA: Harvard University Press.

Pinker, S. (1989). *Learnability and cognition: The acquisition of argument structure*. Cambridge, MA: MIT Press.

Pinker, S. (1994). How could a child use verb syntax to learn verb semantics? *Lingua*, **92**, 377–410.

Plunkett, K., & Marchman, V. (1993). From rote learning to system building: Acquiring verb morphology in children and connectionist nets. *Cognition*, **48**, 21–69.

Poulin, D., & Forbes, J. N. (2002). Toddlers' attention to intentions-in-action in learning novel action words. *Developmental Psychology*, **38**, 104–114.

Poulin-Dubois, D., & Forbes, J. N. (2006). Word, intentions, and action: A two-tiered model of action word learning. In K. Hirsh-Pasek & R. Golinkoff (Eds.), *Action meets word: How children learn verbs* (pp. 262–285). New York: Oxford University Press.

Rescorla, L. A. (1980). Overextension in early language development. *Journal of Child Language*, **7**, 321–335.

Reznick, J. S., Corley, R., & Robinson, J. (1997). A longitudinal twin study of intelligence in the second year. *Monographs of the Society for Research in Child Development*, **62**(1, Serial No. 249).

Rice, M. L., & Bode, J. (1993). GAPS in the verb lexicons of children with specific language impairment. *First Language*, **13**, 113–131.

Robinson, B. F., & Mervis, C. B. (1998). Disentangling early language development: Modeling lexical and grammatical acquisition using an extension of case-study methodology. *Developmental Psychology*, **34**, 363–375.

Rollins, P. R., Snow, C., & Willett, J. (1996). Predictors of MLU: Semantic and morphological developments. *First Language*, **16**, 243–259.

Saffran, J. R., & Thiessen, E. D. (2007). Domain-general learning capacities. In E. Hoff & M. Shatz (Eds.), *Blackwell handbook of language development* (pp. 68–86). Oxford, UK: Blackwell Publishing.

Sandhofer, C. M., & Smith, L. B. (2000). Counting nouns and verbs in the input: Differential frequencies, different kinds of learning? *Journal of child language*, **27**, 561–585.

Shirai, Y. (1998). The emergence of tense-aspect morphology in Japanese: Universal predisposition? *First Language*, **18**, 281–309.

Smiley, P., & Huttenlocher, J. (1995). Conceptual development and the child's early words for events, objects, and persons. In M. Tomasello & W. Merriman (Eds.), *Beyond names for things: Young children's acquisition of verbs* (pp. 21–61). Hillsdale, NJ: Lawrence Erlbaum.

Smith, C., & Sachs, J. (1990). Cognition and the verb lexicon in early lexical development. *Applied Psycholiguistics*, **11**, 409–424.

Smith, L. (1999). Children's noun learning: How general learning processes make specialized learning mechanisms. In B. MacWhinney (Ed.), *The emergence of language* (pp. 29–80). Hillsdale, NJ: Erlbaum.

Smith, L. (2000). Learning how to learn words: An associative crane. In R. Golinkoff, K. Hirsh-Pasek, & L. Bloom (Eds.), *Becoming a word learner: A debate on lexical acquisition* (pp. 51–80). New York: Oxford University Press.

Snedeker, J., & Gleitman, L. R. (2004). Why it is hard to label our concepts. In G. Hall & S. Waxman (Eds.), *Weaving a lexicon* (pp. 257–293). Cambridge, MA: MIT Press.

Snyder, W. (2007). *Child language: The parametric approach.* Oxford, UK: Oxford University Press.

Stromswold, K. (1996). Analyzing children's spontaneous speech. In D. McDaniel, C. McKee, & H. S. Cairns (Eds.), *Methods for assessing children's syntax* (pp. 23–54). Cambridge, MA: MIT Press.

Theakston, A., Lieven, E., Pine, J., & Rowland, C. (2001). The role of performance limitations in the acquisition of verb argument structure: An alternative account. *Journal of Child Language*, **28**, 127–152.

Theakston, A. L., Lieven, E. V. M., Pine, J. M., & Rowland, C. F. (2004). Semantic generality, input frequency and the acquisition of syntax. *Journal of Child Language*, **31**, 61–99.

Theakston, A. L., Lieven, E., & Tomasello, M. (2003). The role of the input in the acquisition of third person singular verbs in English. *Journal of Speech, Language, and Hearing Research*, **46**, 863–877.

Thompson, S. A., & Hopper, P. J. (2001). Transitivity, clause structure, and argument structure: Evidence from conversation. In J. Bybee & P. Hopper (Eds.), *Frequency and the emergence of linguistic structure* (pp. 27–60). Amsterdam, the Netherlands: John Benjamins.

Tomasello, M. (1992). *First verbs: A case study of early grammatical development.* Cambridge, UK: Cambridge University Press.

Tomasello, M. (2000). Do young children have adult syntactic competence? *Cognition*, **74**, 209–253.

Tomasello, M., & Akhtar, N. (2003). What paradox? A response to Naigles (2002). *Cognition*, **88**, 317–323.

Tomasello, M., & Kruger, A. (1992). Joint attention on actions: Acquiring verbs in ostensive and non-ostensive contexts. *Journal of Child Language*, **19**, 311–333.

Tomasello, M., & Merriman, W. (1995). *Beyond names for things: Young children's acquisition of verbs.* Hillsdale, NJ: Erlbaum.

Tomasello, M., & Stahl, D. (2004). Sampling children's spontaneous speech: How much is enough? *Journal of Child Language*, **31**, 101–121.

Valian, V. (1990). Null subjects: A problem for parameter-setting models of language acquisition. *Cognition*, **35**, 105–122.

Valian, V., Prasada, S., & Scarpa, J. (2006). Direct object predictability: Effects on young children's imitation of sentences. *Journal of Child Language*, **33**, 247–269.

Vasilyeva, M., Waterfall, H., & Huttenlocher, J. (2008). Emergence of syntax: Commonalities and differences across children. *Developmental Science*, **11**, 84–97.

Vendler, Z. (1972). *Res cogitans: An essay in rational psychology.* Ithaca, NY: Cornell University Press.

Wagner, L. (2002). Aspectual influences on early tense comprehension. *Journal of Child Language*, **28**, 661–682.

ACKNOWLEDGMENTS

This research was supported in part by the Large Research Grant Program of the University of Connecticut.

We thank Cynthia Fisher, James Magnuson, and our reviewers for their constructive comments on previous versions of the manuscript. We are also grateful to Danielle Popp, Roberta Golinkoff, Aylin Küntay, Marilyn Shatz, Yuriko Oshima-Takane, Lars Bergman, and Whitney Tabor for helpful discussions regarding the work. This research would not have been possible without the dedication of the parents who kept these diaries of their children's first verbs. Special thanks go to Jennifer Coughlan, Eliane Ramos, and Ashley Maltempo for their assistance during data collection and manuscript preparation.

COMMENTARY

FLEXIBILITY IN THE SEMANTICS AND SYNTAX OF CHILDREN'S EARLY VERB USE

Michael Tomasello and Silke Brandt

Objects are boring; they just sit there. Events and actions are where the action is—literally. That is why it is so puzzling that probably 90% of all of the work done on children's early word learning focuses on nouns, and why the current monograph on children's acquisition of verbs is so welcome.

IN PRAISE OF VERBS

Linguistic communication almost always concerns events, actions, or states of affairs. Declaratives or informatives invite the listener to attend to some event, action, or state of affairs, and imperatives or directives enjoin the listener to do something to bring about a desired action or state of affairs. Thus, even when young children are using object labels as single word utterances, from the point of view of the communicative intention as a whole there is almost always some underlying event or action at issue. When the infant exclaims "Airplane!" she is exhorting her mother to attend to it or to notice its presence, and when the infant requests "Juice!" she is rousing her mother into action to satisfy her desire. One could argue that the appropriate gloss of such utterances is something along the lines of "*Look* at the airplane!" (or "The airplane *is there*!") and "*Get* me some juice!" The action or state of affairs intended, and its corresponding verb, is implicit; the utterance is what has been called a holophrase.

The one potential exception is naming objects. But naming objects is actually a kind of metalinguistic speech act. It is not using language but rather "mentioning" it, mostly teaching it. Western, middle-class parents do this with some regularity with their children, and their children learn the names and then show off by using them in return. But in many other cultures the pedagogical or demonstrative naming of objects is a very rare type of speech act and plays very little role in the acquisition of language.

113

And even in Western, middle-class culture parents only rarely explicitly teach words other than object labels. With verbs and other types of words, children must in almost all cases learn them within the ongoing flow of social interaction and discourse—on their own, so to speak—based on their understanding of the intentional actions of others in the social interaction. For example, young children are able to infer the referent action of a novel verb even when they hear it only as a directive to act or as an anticipation of an impending action even if they never actually see the referent action at all—based on the adult's accompanying behavior and context (Tomasello, 1992, 1995, 2001). This social–cognitive complexity in the acquisition process is another reason why the acquisition of verbs is so interesting.

From a semantic point of view, events and their corresponding verbs are also much more complex conceptually than objects and their corresponding nouns (setting aside for the moment nouns for other kinds of referents, as children's early nouns are mostly used for concrete objects). Even the very earliest verbs that children learn and use vary in whether they are causative or not (e.g., *give* vs. *have*), in whether they designate results or not (e.g., *clean* the table vs. *wipe* the table), in whether they designate manner of motion or not (e.g., *roll* vs. *move*), in whether they are defined by a particular objects or not (e.g., *hammer* vs. *hit*), in whether they are about specific bodily movements or more abstract changes of state (e.g., *lick*, involving specific movements of the tongue, vs. *cut*, involving very different actions depending on what is cut, from the lawn to a finger)—not to mention all of the different aspects of actions that may be designated grammatically (ongoing events vs. completed events vs. impending events vs. past events vs. future events, etc.). Indeed, Gentner (1982) famously stressed that in many cases it is difficult to know how to conceptually "package" the ongoing flow of experience into discrete events, as referred to by verbs, at all.

Further in this direction is the fact that events and verbs always involve one or more participants, typically designated linguistically by nouns and not in any way "given" by the phenomenal event itself (indeed, some verbs can be used so as to highlight different participants on different occasions of use, e.g., *John broke the vase*, with two participants indicated, vs. *The vase broke*, with only one indicated). And so, in a sense, events incorporate objects but not the reverse. And this is the final way in which verbs are especially important and interesting in the study of child language acquisition. As stressed by researchers from all theoretical backgrounds (e.g., Pinker, 1989; Tomasello, 1992), verbs have as part of their very meaning the participants involved (paraphrasing William Blake's famous observation, if there is dancing there must be a dancer). This makes the acquisition of verbs already a step on the way to grammatical competence, as the learning of verbs involves the kind of verb–argument (event–participant) structures that form the backbone of mature sentence structure.

It is thus for all of these reasons that the current monograph is so welcome in the field. Verbs are arguably the most complex and important type of word in early language development, and they have been sorely neglected (see the papers in Hirsh-Pasek & Golinkoff, 2006; Tomasello & Merriman, 1995, for some notable exceptions).

IN PRAISE OF THE DIARY METHOD

Researchers in other areas of developmental psychology sometimes puzzle over the use of parent diaries in the study of language acquisition. But there are very good reasons for the use of this method, and the current monograph involves the innovative extension of using multiple parent–child pairs.

The basic problem is that children talk too much. A child is awake and talking around 10 hr/day, 7 days/week, but the normal sampling regime in language acquisition research is a maximum of one of those 70 hr/week. This is a sample of 1–2% of what the child says. The reason researchers do not sample more is because it takes from 10 to 20 hr to transcribe 1 hr of taped conversation. But, despite this good practical reason, this 1–2% sample is inherently limited, potentially biased in all the ways that small samples may be biased in all scientific inquiry, and it very likely misses completely most low-frequency phenomena. And so, for example, it has been quantitatively demonstrated that with a small sample estimating the age at which the child acquires low-frequency linguistic items or structure is highly unreliable (Rowland & Fletcher, 2006; Tomasello & Stahl, 2004).

Diaries have their own limitations of course. Most obviously, they prototypically involve only one child—limiting external validity—and parents are not trained scientific observers. But with the collection of multiple diaries of comparable children—again, an innovation of the current study—the first problem is to some degree overcome. And, in terms of the limitations of parents as observers, it has been established by researchers using the MacArthur Communicative Development Inventory (a paper-and-pencil assessment of children's vocabulary filled out by parents) that parents are actually highly reliable at recording their child's overt behaviors (Fenson et al., 1994). This is especially true if parents are directed what to look for. And the current study did an especially good job of this by focusing parents' attention on a smallish number of specific verbs that their children might be using.

Finally, there is one further advantage to diaries that is often not stressed. Because the parent is recording basically everything (of some designated focal phenomena), one can conclude with reasonable certainty when the child does *not* do something, which can never be concluded with small- or even medium-sized samples. In the study of language acquisition, this is often important since one of the key issues is the degree to which children use their early language flexibly and productively, and to determine that we must know not only what they have done but also what they might have done but did not. And indeed, the current monograph is concerned precisely with the issues of flexibility and productivity, and so the diary method is especially appropriate.

FLEXIBILITY IN EARLY VERB USE

The data of the current monograph provide us with by far the most complete, quantitative picture in the literature of how English-speaking children learn and use their early verbs. Within the limitations of the diary method (including the fact that the researchers focused parents on a subset of 34 preselected target verbs),[1] we now have at our disposal a vast and important array of new facts.

Flexibility in Verb Use: Pragmatics and Semantics

Parents kept the diary until they had recorded 10 actual instances of use of each targeted verb, that is, 10 utterances containing the verb in question. Across all of the verbs used by all of the children, the average time it took for the 10 instances to be produced by the child was a bit over 1 month. Pragmatically, the children used about half of their verbs either as commands or as descriptions only; the other half were used in both functions. Foreshadowing an issue that will come up later with regard to syntax, we do not know in which of these instances children heard their parents using the verb in both pragmatic functions, and so we do not know if children are simply following the adult use or doing something more creative in using these pragmatic functions with particular verbs. And because there are no experiments in the literature addressing this question, we simply do not know.

From the point of view of semantics, the current monograph found that the children used their newly acquired verbs relatively flexibly from relatively early. This fact was not a foregone conclusion. Although research has shown that children use their object labels in fairly flexible ways from early on (Harris, Barrett, Jones, & Brookes, 1988), a number of different naturalistic observations have provided examples of young children using verbs and other types of words in more context bound ways for some time (e.g., Gopnik, 1988; Tomasello, 1992). But it has never been clear whether those are unrepresentative examples or whether they might reflect some more systematic difference with object labels.

In the current study, children did not confine their use of verbs to a single, narrowly defined action type; they used almost 40% of their verbs to refer to different action types (e.g., a person coming vs. a TV show coming)—and this number would undoubtedly be higher if "different action type" had been defined more loosely. These new uses occurred, on average, after about four uses of the verb in question. And children quite often used their verbs for different actors and patients of these actions as well (whether these were lexically realized or not). Thus, for something around three quarters of their verbs, children referred to events involving different actors on different occasions, and about the same proportion were used to refer to events involving different patients of the actions. In both cases, the new actors and/or patients occurred after around three uses of the verb in question. Although we cannot be sure if the children are following adult usage or are being more creative in their semantic extensions in all cases, other diary studies in the past have noted many cases of creative extensions to novel referents (e.g., Bowerman, 1982).

Given that children use much of their early language in recurrent social situations and routines, these percentages seem fairly high, and they would seem to refute any proposal that children are inflexible in their early use of verbs to refer to events and actions in the world. One might ask how this flexibility compares with children's early use of object labels, but the answer is that we do not know because we do not have quite such detailed data in this case. There are some diary studies (especially Dromi, 1987) that have focused on the acquisition of object labels in enough detail to provide some relevant data for comparison, but since the two types of word are so different semantically, it is difficult to think how such a comparison could be done quantitatively. In any case, the general conclusion would seem to be that English-speaking children use both their early nouns and their early verbs in reasonably flexible ways to refer to all kinds of objects and events in the world.

This having been said, it is unclear that—despite the literature review in the current monograph—anyone espousing any theory of word learning would predict that children in the second half of their 2nd year of life would still be using any kinds of words in highly context bound ways. Virtually all of the proposals for early context bound use have focused on the first half of the 2nd year of life or even earlier.

Flexibility in Verb Use: Syntax

The most contentious issue in the monograph is children's flexibility and productivity in using their early verbs syntactically. We deal first with the issue of flexibility, which, in the current context, means children using their verbs in syntactically diverse contexts. In the following section, we will deal with the issue of productivity, which, in the current context, means children using their verbs in syntactic contexts that go beyond those in which they have heard them being used. Productivity is an especially contentious issue as it involves the degree to which young children's language is underlain by abstract, lexically general, linguistic categories and constructions (rules). But the two issues are tied together; hence, let us first sort them out a bit.

Several authors, including ourselves, have proposed that children do not have innate and abstract grammatical categories that apply equally across all words as part of their beginning linguistic competence—the basic Chomskian proposal. Instead, much of their early grammatical competence revolves around specific verbs or other items such as pronouns (Lieven, Pine, & Baldwin, 1997; Tomasello, 1992, 2000, 2003). Thus, children begin with lexically specific constructions—some of which have been called verb island constructions because they revolve around verbs—with only local, lexically specific abstractions. In this theory, if the young child says "Doggie kiss me," the item-based construction involved might be something like *kisser* KISS *kissee*, without reference to such verb-general things as agents and patients, much less subjects and objects. With this item-based construction, the child could learn a new object label and immediately use it as either "kisser" or "kissee" productively, without hearing others do this, based on an understanding of all the items involved. But what she could not do is to learn a new verb, say *hug*, and immediately make an analogy to *kiss* and use it with a "hugger" and a "hugee" without having heard others do it. Each lexically specific construction is a structural island.

The evidence for this proposal comes from both naturalistic observations and experiments. Many studies of natural samples of children's early language show restricted use of words and lexically specific schemas (e.g., Lieven, Behrens, Speares, & Tomasello, 2003; Lieven et al., 1997), and this restricted use has been taken to reflect a relative lack of lexically general categories and constructions that can be used totally productively. But most comparable to the current data is Tomasello's (1992) original diary study. In that study there were two basic findings relevant to issues of verb flexibility and productivity.

The first was that the majority of this diary child's early verbs were used in fairly simple sentence frames, often only one frame per verb, and different verbs most often had different frames—suggesting that they were each an island and not very flexible. These are the data that the current monograph addresses, and, as noted by the authors, the data of the two diary studies are generally very comparable, once one adopts the same coding criteria for both. The outcome is the story of a glass either half empty or half full, depending on one's perspective. Here is a quick summary of the relevant data from the current monograph (based on the diaries of the eight children that were fully analyzed).

- Of the few verbs the children used at 18 months, only 15% were used in more than one sentence frame. At 20 months, 44% of the children's verbs were used in more than one sentence frame. At 24 months, 55% of the children's verbs were used in more than one sentence frame.

- Across the entire period of diary collection, children used 31% of their verbs with more than one lexically expressed subject, and 43% of their verbs with more than one lexically expressed object.

- Across the entire period of diary collection, children used only 16% of their verbs with more than one morphological form (e.g., present or past tense).

- Of the transitive verbs that children used over the course of the study, 35% were used with both subject and object lexically expressed (56% were used as one word utterances or with only one argument expressed).

- Of the intransitive verbs that children used over the course of the study, 30% were used with the subject lexically expressed (53% were used as one word utterances).

- From the perspective of the sentence frames, at 24 months of age, three of the eight children did not have a single frame that they used with five verbs or more, one child had one such frame, and four children had three to five such frames.

Whether one considers this syntactic flexibility or not depends on one's point of view. The authors of the current monograph—taking as background general claims of lexical specificity in early grammars—think it is pretty flexible.

But the alternative interpretation of these kinds of data by proponents of lexical specificity has typically used as background the expectation that children's language is structured by a set of abstract syntactic categories and constructions that apply across all relevant lexical items equally. In this context, one wonders why children use about one third of their transitive and intransitive verbs with all of the syntactically required arguments, but the other two thirds without. And why do children at around 2 years of age still use almost half of their verbs in only one sentence frame? And why are there so few sentence frames used across multiple verbs? From this perspective, although children show some flexibility, it does not look even remotely like all of their utterances derive from a set of preexisting, abstract, lexically neutral, syntactic categories, and rules.

Underlying this disagreement about flexibility is really the issue of productivity. In the verb island hypothesis, children may be as flexible as you like in their use of particular verbs in syntactic frames and morphological paradigms—so long as they have heard all of these uses in the language around them. With each verb, they learn various ways of talking from the discourse interactions they have with adults—that is, for each verb separately. And so, in Tomasello's (1992) diary, a paradigm example is *cut* versus *draw*. *Cut* was used by Tomasello's child in only one basic sentence frame, whereas *draw* (learned at about the same time and having somewhat similar semantics) was used in many different ones. The general explanation is that, for whatever reason, the child either heard or attended to many different syntactic uses of *draw*, but not so for *cut*. Thus, flexibility of use for a particular verb is purely a function of the language the child has heard and attended to with that verb, along with her motivation for speaking about these kinds of events.

And so flexibility with particular verbs does not signal lexically general productivity across all verbs, unless one has evidence that the flexibility is due to a child's creative generalization and not simply to a reproduction of adult flexibility with each particular verb individually. Children will become productive in all kinds of ways at some point—including across verbs and constructions—it is just that initially they are not. This is important because it speaks to process. If children begin lexically based and become more productive only gradually, then the likelihood is that the process is not one of activating innate syntactic categories and rules, but rather one of constructing ever more general syntactic categories and rules on the basis of general cognitive processes (e.g., statistical learning, analogy) and input from mature language users.

PRODUCTIVITY IN EARLY VERB USE

Syntactic productivity is thus the key theoretical issue. Indeed, in the first draft of this monograph (which we reviewed) the entire focus was on productivity. The theoretical reason for this derives mainly from Chomsky's poverty of the stimulus argument. If from the beginning children go beyond the language they have heard in creative and productive ways, this suggests that they have preexisting abstract categories and schemas (or rules) that generate their early language. This is the argument that the authors tried to make in the first draft. But the reviewers simply noted that without any data about what language the children had heard, one can talk about flexibility but not about productivity. One cannot say that children are going beyond what they have heard if one does not know what they have heard. That syntactic productivity is indeed the issue these authors wish to push is evident in their quote near the end of the monograph:

> These findings are more consistent with the generativist view of child language acquisition (e.g., Chomsky, 1981; Gleitman & Fisher, 2002) than with the positions that children are conservative language users and that 2-year-olds do not have abstract syntax (e.g., Goldberg, 1998; Lieven, 2006; Tomasello, 2000). (p. 107)[2]

But, to reiterate, in the original verb island formulation, as well as in other item-based approaches, children are syntactically productive—but only in limited ways constrained within their item-based constructions. Thus, as alluded to above, from as early as they are combining words, if one teaches a child a novel noun in an experiment (e.g., *the wug*), they immediately stick it into the syntactic slot of many of their existing verbs and predicate terms straightaway, saying such productive things as "Wug gone" and "Find wug"—even though they have never before heard *wug* combined with any other word (Tomasello, Akhtar, & Rekau, 1997). Early in development most sentence frames are structured by verbs (like *gone* and *find*), each of which fills new words into its argument slots freely and productively. Hence, children are productive with their language in some ways from near the beginning of multiword speech.

It is just that transfer of structure across verb island constructions does not happen as the result of the pregiven and abstract categories of formal linguistics but develops as a result of both what the child hears and her developing generalizations across initially very low-scope schemas. This is illustrated by another analysis performed in Tomasello's (1992) diary study. The logic was this. Suppose the child learned one of her verbs in a full transitive construction, for example, saying many things of the form *x* FIND *y*. If this construction was fully abstract and verb general, one would expect to see her using other verbs in the same frame pretty soon after, that is, given the opportunity to do so. But that is not what the data showed. If one looked at the development of the sentence frames used with a particular verb across time, the child added grammatical complexity only gradually and incrementally for each verb separately. It almost never happened that a verb that was at one point used in a simple sentence frame all of a sudden was used in a more complex one, for example, based on some kind of transfer from another verb that had recently been used in this more complex frame. The summary statement was as follows: By far the best predictor of this child's use of a given verb on a given day was not her use of other verbs on that same day, but rather her use of that same verb on immediately preceding days. Hence, the evidence here was that the overall developmental pattern suggested initial syntactic independence for each verb.

121

No comparable analysis was performed on individual children in the current study. The analyses of the individual children (displayed in Figures 11–19) basically showed the following. In terms of the number of sentence frames used with each verb (flexibility), across time two children showed U-shaped development (Heather, Elaine); two children showed a several month period with no flexibility followed by a relatively rapid increase in flexibility (Carl, Sam); and the other four children showed relatively quick flexibility early on. This kind of analysis does not look for any kind of transfer across sentence frames. In another recent study, based on samples of children's speech (not on a thorough diary), Ninio (2006) claims to find such transfer. But herein lies the rub. Even in this case one cannot claim anything about transfer or productivity if one does not know what language the children have heard, or how their other cognitive abilities are developing. Hence, it could be that once a child's parents hear her using transitive sentences with one verb, this encourages them to use transitive sentences more often, or more saliently, with other verbs. Or perhaps the child's working memory is expanding during this time, making the individual acquisition of more complex verb island constructions possible for the first time.

The fundamental point is that one cannot investigate productivity directly without knowing the language the child has heard. Researchers have therefore considered it of special importance when children overgeneralize and say things like "She giggled me" (Bowerman, 1982)—on the assumption that this sentence must be generated by a productive schema, as the child would never have heard such a sentence with that verb in their everyday linguistic environment (these productive errors usually do not occur before age 3 years; Pinker, 1989). The other approach is, of course, experiments. We and others have performed literally dozens of experiments in which we teach children a novel verb (e.g., *tamming*) in various ways and see if they then use it in existing constructions like the transitive or intransitive or passive—when given multiple opportunities and motivation to do so. The outcome, as the authors of the monograph note, is that children younger than 2.5–3 years of age show very little productivity with newly learned novel verbs—even though older children show much productivity with these same verbs learned in these same ways (see Tomasello, 2000, 2003, for reviews).

The authors of the current monograph focus their critique only on the production experiments, but we and others have also done similar experiments tapping the child's comprehension (e.g., to see if children can understand who is doing what to whom in "The dog is tamming the cat") (e.g., Akhtar & Tomasello, 1997; Chan, Lieven, & Tomasello, 2009; Dittmar, Abbot-Smith, Lieven, & Tomasello, 2008a), as well as structural priming experiments using familiar English verbs (e.g., Savage, Lieven, Theakston,

& Tomasello, 2003). In all of these paradigms we are testing for productivity across verb island constructions in the absence of relevant input—suggesting the existence of abstract, verb-general schemas—but in all cases the finding is of very little syntactic productivity before about 2.5–3 years of age. The current authors focus instead on a recent preferential looking study with English-speaking children by Gertner, Fisher, and Eisengart (2006), supposedly showing syntactic productivity in children under 2 years of age. Leaving aside the question of how to interpret the results of a looking discrimination in terms of the nature of underlying representations, that study used a training technique before the children entered the experiment that taught them key aspects of the construction (i.e., it used the same actors and associated nouns in both training and testing in the same semantic roles). When German-speaking children were tested without such an initial training period, they did not show any syntactic productivity at this young age (Dittmar, Abbot-Smith, Lieven, & Tomasello, 2008b). And so it seems very clear, to us at least, that the experimental data show a consistent lack of syntactic productivity in young children across several different methodologies, in both comprehension and production, using both novel and familiar verbs. One can always criticize experiments as not being ecologically valid, but in this case there are many different methodologies involved.

The main point is that there is no evidence in the current monograph for syntactic productivity in 1- and 2-year-old children—in the sense of generalizing across verbs to create verb-general syntactic constructions—because we do not know what language they have heard being used around them, and there is no other indirect evidence either. Children are flexible from the beginning, as they learn from adults multiple frames for a given verb. And they are productive in the limited sense that they can freely substitute participants for one another in the syntactic slots of each verb-specific syntactic frame individually, thus creating schemas such as x FIND y. But based on Tomasello's (1992) longitudinal analysis failing to find transfer across verbs, and on the extensive experimental literature in which children remain conservative with their syntactic constructions for some time, our own conclusion is that the grammatical organization underlying children's early linguistic competence is not abstract and rule-based, but rather is concrete and item-based—leading to highly constrained productivity.

Perhaps one reason for the slow buildup of productivity in young children's early syntax is that to make generalizations across such things as verb island constructions children must make complex analogies between complex structures (e.g., aligning agents with agents and patients with patients in utterances with different transitive verbs). The age at which they seem to do this most readily in nonlinguistic domains corresponds fairly well with the age at which they seem to be doing it with their language (see Gentner &

123

Markman, 1997). And it is perhaps worth noting as well that psycholinguistic research has shown that even adults' representations of argument structures are still fairly closely tied to specific lexical items (e.g., Trueswell & Tanenhaus, 1994).

CONCLUSION

The current monograph is extremely valuable and advances the field significantly in multiple ways. By exploiting the level of detail and thoroughness of the diary method—and then employing it across multiple children—the authors were able to collect data on children's early acquisition of verbs that enabled all kinds of quantitative assessments simply not possible in other kinds of studies. We now know new and important facts about children's semantic flexibility with verbs in early development that will help us to better formulate theories of lexical development that are inclusive of all word types. And we now know new and important facts about children's syntactic flexibility with verbs that will help us to formulate better theories of how children come to generate and grammatically structure their early multiword productions. And although we have been critical in this commentary about the claims of certain kinds of syntactic productivity in the current data set—we actually believe that that is impossible without experiments—nevertheless, as the authors point out in several places, flexibility is a precondition for productivity, and so the investigation of children's flexibility is a very important first step in figuring out how children ultimately construct their abstract syntactic constructions.

NOTES

1. The authors' selection of verbs to focus on is well justified, except for the exclusion of three fairly important early verbs, *make*, *do*, and *have*.

2. Although on p. 109 we get the somewhat contradictory: "One position consistent with our data is that abstract grammatical categories are learned from the input, but the process of learning begins early, before speech production at all or before production of the relevant linguistic frame or construction."

References

Akhtar, N., & Tomasello, M. (1997). Young children's productivity with word order and word morphology. *Developmental Psychology*, **33**, 952–965.

Bowerman, M. (1982). Starting to talk worse: Clues to language acquisition from children's late speech errors. In S. Strauss & R. Stavy (Eds.), *U-shaped behavioral growth* (pp. 101–146). New York: Academic Press.

Chan, A., Lieven, E., & Tomasello, M. (2009). Children's understanding of the agent-patient relations in the transitive construction: Cross-linguistic comparisons between Cantonese, German and English. *Cognitive Linguistics*, **20**, 267–300.

Dittmar, M., Abbot-Smith, K., Lieven, E., & Tomasello, M. (2008a). German children's comprehension of word order and case marking in causative sentences. *Child Development*, **79**(4), 1152–1167.

Dittmar, M., Abbot-Smith, K., Lieven, E., & Tomasello, M. (2008b). Young German children's early syntactic competence: A preferential looking study. *Developmental Science*, **23**, 48–66.

Dromi, E. (1987). *Early lexical development*. Cambridge, UK: Cambridge University Press.

Fenson, L., Dale, P. S., Reznick, J. S., Bates, E., Thal, D., & Pethick, S. (1994). Variability in early communicative development. *Monographs of the Society of Research in Child Development*, **59**(5).

Gentner, D. (1982). Why nouns are learned before verbs: Linguistic relativity versus natural partitioning. In S. A. Kuczaj (Ed.), *Language development: Vol. 2. Language, thought and culture* (pp. 301–334). Hillsdale, NJ: Lawrence Erlbaum.

Gentner, D., & Markman, A. B. (1997). Structure mapping in analogy and similarity. *American Psychologist*, **52**, 45–56.

Gertner, Y., Fisher, C., & Eisengart, J. (2006). Learning words and rules: Abstract knowledge of word order in early sentence comprehension. *Psychological Science*, **17**(8), 684–691.

Gopnik, A. (1988). Three types of early word: Social words, cognitive-relational words and names and their relation to cognitive development. *First Language*, **8**, 49–70.

Harris, M., Barrett, M., Jones, D., & Brookes, S. (1988). Linguistic input and early word meaning. *Journal of Child Language*, **15**, 77–94.

Hirsh-Pasek, K., & Golinkoff, R. M. (Eds.). (2006). *Action meets word: How children learn verbs*. New York: Oxford University Press.

Lieven, E., Behrens, H., Speares, J., & Tomasello, M. (2003). Early syntactic creativity: A usage-based approach. *Journal of Child Language*, **30**(2), 333–367.

Lieven, E., Pine, J., & Baldwin, G. (1997). Lexically based learning and early grammatical development. *Journal of Child Language*, **24**(1), 187–219.

Ninio, A. (2006). *Language and the learning curve: A new theory of syntactic development*. Oxford, UK: Oxford University Press.

Pinker, S. (1989). *Learnability and cognition: The acquisition of argument structure*. Cambridge, MA: MIT Press.

Rowland, C. F., & Fletcher, S. L. (2006). The effect of sampling on estimates of lexical specificity and error rates. *Journal of Child Language*, **33**(4), 859–877.

Savage, C., Lieven, E., Theakston, A., & Tomasello, M. (2003). Testing the abstractness of children's linguistic representations: Lexical and structural priming of syntactic constructions in young children. *Developmental Science*, **6**(5), 557–567.

Tomasello, M. (1992). *First verbs: A case study of early grammatical development*. New York: Cambridge University Press.

Tomasello, M. (1995). Pragmatic contexts for early verb learning. In M. Tomasello & W. Merriman (Eds.), *Beyond names for things: Young children's acquisition of verbs* (pp. 115–146). Hillsdale, NJ: Lawrence Erlbaum.

Tomasello, M. (2000). Do young children have adult syntactic competence? *Cognition*, **74**(3), 209–253.

Tomasello, M. (2001). Perceiving intentions and learning words in the second year of life. In M. Bowerman & S. Levinson (Eds.), *Language acquisition and conceptual development* (pp. 132–158). Cambridge, UK: Cambridge University Press.

Tomasello, M. (2003). *Constructing a language. A usage-based theory of language acquisition*. Cambridge, MA: Harvard University Press.

Tomasello, M., Akhtar, N., Dodson, K., & Rekau, L. (1997). Differential productivity in young children's use of nouns and verbs. *Journal of Child Language*, **24**, 373–387.

Tomasello, M., & Merriman, W. (Eds.). (1995). *Beyond names for things: Young children's acquisition of verbs*. Hillsdale, NJ: Lawrence Erlbaum.

Tomasello, M., & Stahl, D. (2004). Sampling children's spontaneous speech: How much is enough? *Journal of Child Language*, **31**(1), 101–121.

Trueswell, J. C., & Tanenhaus, M. K. (1994). Toward a lexicalist framework of constraint-based syntactic ambiguity resolution. In C. Clifton Jr., L. Frazier, & K. Rayner (Eds.), *Perspectives on sentence processing* (pp. 155–179). Hillsdale, NJ: Lawrence Erlbaum.

COMMENTARY

LEARNING FROM INFANTS' FIRST VERBS

Sandra R. Waxman

Across the centuries, people have been fascinated with infants' first words. This fascination is not a special characteristic of parents of young children, developmental psychologists, or psycholinguistics. Instead, this fascination is widespread, and infants' first words can serve as entry points to heated discussions of topics as far ranging as innate knowledge, the nature of intelligence, and the development of national character.

Thanks to the writings of the Greek historian Herodotus, we can trace the fascination with infants' first words to the time of Psammetichus, an Egyptian pharoah who reigned in the seventh-century BC. According to legend, Psammetichus held firmly to the belief that the Egyptians were the most ancient people in the world, but this was disputed hotly by the Phrygians, who argued that in fact they were the originals. To settle this dispute (and to claim the Egyptian people their rightful place), Psammetichus developed a passionate interest in infants' first words, a passion that stemmed from a desire to discover the origin of human language and that led him to conduct the first known experiment on language development in children. Apparently, he somehow managed to bring two newborn infants to a shepherd, living alone among his flock of sheep. The protocol for this proto-experiment was simple and clear: it was the shepherd's responsibility to feed and care for the infants, to make sure that they heard absolutely no human language, and to wait patiently and listen carefully for the infants' first words. The hypothesis was equally clear: he reasoned that in the absence of any linguistic input, the first word uttered by these infants would reveal which language was the origin of all human languages. As it turned out, the shepherd reported that the first word uttered by the children was "becos," a word they uttered repeatedly and excitedly with their arms outstretched. When Psammetichus learned that "becos" was the Phrygian word for bread, he accepted for the first time that Phrygian, and not Egyptian, was the original language of humankind.

127

In the 21st century, our interest in infants' first words remains strong, but stems from a different source. We are no longer consumed with discovering which language is the lingua franca of humankind, but instead with what infants' first words can reveal about the nature of the human mind and how it is shaped by experience.

In their monograph, Naigles, Hoff, and Vear (2009) provide an outstanding example of how a careful analysis of infants' first words, and especially their first verbs, can inform current theories and debates in language acquisition. Focusing on eight infants, ranging from 16 to 20 months at the start of the investigation, the monograph traces each infant's first uses of their earliest acquired verbs. The diary records, compiled with the apparently tireless support of the infants' mothers, offer a rich depiction of the pragmatic, semantic, and syntactic properties of infants' early verb productions. Infants' productions, and the contexts in which they occur, then serve as an empirical base against which competing hypotheses about the flexibility and productivity of infants' early-acquired verbs can be tested.

RICHLY DESCRIPTIVE

This monograph fills an important niche. In essence, it represents the first of what we might call a "focused diary design." It provides an important counterpoint to more traditional diary studies, illustrating that the diary of any one child, no matter how comprehensive, cannot tell us everything we need to know. After all, although the eight children included in this monograph were drawn from a rather homogenous population (e.g., raised in middle- to upper-middle-class families by majority culture, stay-at-home mothers) and although even within this population they represent the midrange along a continuum of approaches to language acquisition (e.g., those who produced too much or too little were excluded), their diaries nonetheless vary considerably, revealing a range of distinct approaches to early verb learning. Importantly, then, this richly descriptive monograph serves as a resource to which we can turn to later to pursue a host of questions.

DIARY DATA *GUIDED BY* AND *APPLIED TO* THEORY

Another outstanding feature of this monograph is its strong commitment to theory. The data were guided by, and then applied to, theory. In addition, the monograph offers insight into the tight coupling between method and coding on the one hand, and theory and interpretation on the other.

CENTRAL TENDENCIES AND INDIVIDUAL DIFFERENCES

The analyses of these eight diaries not only uncover developmental patterns within the group as a whole, but also identify potential individual differences. This underscores the importance of bearing in mind that not all children go about the process of language production in the same way. An analysis of group patterns and means offers evidence of the central tendencies, but beneath the surface, it is often possible to discern different individual styles (Bloom, 1973; Nelson, 1973). Attending to these individual differences is instructive, and in the case of this monograph, it permits the authors to describe different developmental paths. It also underscores that although children may approach the task of language acquisition with a universal set of linguistic competences, these alone do not determine the child's path of production. This path is also shaped by linguistic character-istics of the input (e.g., Greek vs. English), the amount of input (rich vs. sparse), and personalities of the individual child (cautious vs. intrepid) (Gleitman, Cassidy, Papafragou, Nappa, & Trueswell, 2005; Gleitman & Fisher, 2005; Huttenlocher, Vasilyeva, Cymmerman, & Levine, 2002; Wax-man & Lidz, 2006).

THE MATTERS OF "ABSTRACTNESS" AND "FLEXIBILITY"

The decision to focus on the first 10 uses was motivated by the goal of identifying the breadth of children's first representations of verb use and verb meaning. This is a key question, because there is currently consider-able controversy over the breadth or abstractness of infants' early verb meanings and applications. For example, if an infant produces the verb *wave* in the context of a flag-waving event, what can we say about her rep-resentation? Does she construe the verb narrowly, applying it to flag-waving events only? Does she construe it too abstractly, applying it to any and all events that involve moving one's hand while grasping an object? The au-thors of the monograph approached this question directly, bringing the toddlers' productions to bear on key theoretical perspectives (Fisher, 1996; Hirsh-Pasek & Golinkoff, 2006; Lidz & Gleitman, 2004; Lieven, Behrens, Speares, & Tomasello, 2003; Naigles, 2002; Tomasello, 2000; Waxman & Lidz, 2006).

In addition to recording each infant's first 10 uses of a series of verbs, the mothers and researchers also worked together to record the range of utterances in which the newly produced verbs appeared and the range of situations to which they were applied. The decision to focus on the con-ditions under which the verb was produced is also motivated by theory.

129

At issue here is the question of flexibility of verb use. Of course, although it is not a simple matter to operationalize flexibility, especially with utterances as short as those produced by these very young children, the authors were careful to guide their decisions by theory.

Another strength of the analysis is the authors' efforts to tease apart several (potentially) distinct elements of flexibility (e.g., pragmatic flexibility, semantic flexibility, grammatical flexibility). But there is a wrinkle in this analysis because the kinds of grammatical frames in which a verb can occur are not unrelated to their semantics (Fisher, 1996, 2002; Gleitman, 1990; Lidz, Gleitman, & Gleitman, 2004). As a result, it is important to bear in mind that measures of semantic and grammatical flexibility are, of necessity, not independent.

Although focusing on flexibility and abstractness of early verb use is an important advance, at the same time, it raises several thorny questions of its own. Chief among them, does the child's flexibility of verb use, as measured here, really reveal the abstractness of the underlying grammar? It might, but at this point, and based on the current data, we cannot rule a strong alternative hypothesis: that in using verbs flexibly, children are merely mirroring the input to which they have been exposed (i.e., the various frames in which they have heard these very verbs in the ambient language). After all, if children have indeed been actively processing the input language for more than a year, then by the time they produce their first verbs, they would have heard each of these verbs in many different frames. As a result, we might *expect* them to be flexible even in their first 10 uses. To resolve this important matter, it will be important to search for and analyze children's errors.

What this suggests is that although carefully cataloguing infants' first 10 uses is an important step, it may not take us far enough. The first 10 uses may prove to be too blunt an instrument to resolve some of the finely honed questions of early language acquisition. Still, this first step certainly takes us far enough to see where we should step next.

OPENING THE DOOR TO NEW RESEARCH ENDEAVORS

Certainly, this monograph opens the door to several creative lines of additional research. For example, it highlights the importance of analyzing the input to young children, even before they produce their first verbs, and provides guideposts for the kinds of input analyses that are most likely to bear fruit. It also sets the stage for a careful analysis of how the view we obtain from diary studies and language production in general relates to the view that we obtain from more standard experimental work based on language comprehension.

In addition, the monograph makes clear the importance of a more comprehensive analysis, looking beyond the first 10 uses of these early-produced verbs. How can we best characterize the trajectory of these verbs? Do children exhibit a steep increase, or explosion, in flexibility or abstractness, or is development characterized by a deepening reliance on the early-acquired frames? Finally, it will be important to pursue focused diary studies of infants acquiring languages other than English, focusing especially on languages that differ in theory-relevant ways.

The strongest signature for a "classic-in-the making" is not whether the work answers all of our questions, but whether it offers to carry us forward in our inquiries. There is no doubt that when considering the contribution of Naigles, Hoff, and Vear, the answer is "yes." Thanks to their monograph, we can move beyond asking whether young children are capable of learning verbs. Clearly they are. We can also move beyond asking whether they are capable of representing language and grammar in an abstract or flexible fashion. Apparently they can. Instead, we can now move forward to pinpoint the conditions that best support the acquisition of abstract knowledge and the use of flexible representations, to identify how early in development this abstract knowledge becomes evident, and to discover how quickly it is apprehended when young children encounter a new verb.

ACKNOWLEDGMENT

Preparation of the commentary was supported by NIH HD030410.

References

Bloom, L. (1973). *One word at a time: The use of single-word utterances before syntax.* The Hague: Mouton.

Fisher, C. (1996). Structural limits on verb mapping: The role of analogy in children's interpretations of sentences. *Cognitive Psychology*, **31**, 41–81.

Fisher, C. (2002). Structural limits on verb mapping: The role of abstract structure in 2.5-year-olds' interpretations of novel verbs. *Developmental Science*, **5**, 56–65.

Gleitman, L. R., & Fisher, C. (2005). Universal aspects of word learning. In J. McGilvray (Ed.), *The Cambridge Companion to Chomsky* (pp. 123–142). Cambridge, UK: Cambridge University Press.

Gleitman, L. (1990). The structural sources of verb meanings. *Language Acquisition: A Journal of Developmental Linguistics*, **1**(1), 3–55.

Gleitman, L. R., Cassidy, K., Papafragou, A., Nappa, R., & Trueswell, J. T. (2005). Hard words. *Journal of Language Learning and Development*, **1**, 23–64.

Hirsh-Pasek, K. & Golinkoff, R. (Eds.). (2006). *Action meets word: How children learn verbs.* New York: Oxford University Press.

Huttenlocher, J., Vasilyeva, M., Cymmerman, E., & Levine, S. (2002). Language input and child syntax. *Cognitive Psychology*, **45**, 337–374.

Lidz, J., Gleitman, H., & Gleitman, L. (2004). Kidz in the 'hood: Syntactic bootstrapping and the mental lexicon. In D. G. Hall & S. R. Waxman (Eds.), *Weaving a lexicon* (pp. 603–636). Cambridge, MA: MIT Press.

Lidz, J., & Gleitman, L. (2004). Argument structure and the child's contribution to language learning. *Trends in Cognitive Science*, **8**, 157–161.

Lieven, E., Behrens, H., Speares, J., & Tomasello, M. (2003). Early syntactic creativity: A usage-based approach. *Journal of Child Language*, **30**, 333–367.

Naigles, L. R. (2002). Form is easy, meaning is hard: Resolving a paradox in early child language. *Cognition*, **86**, 157–199.

Naigles, L. R., Hoff, E., & Vear, D. (2009). Flexibility in early verb use: Evidence from a multiple-N diary study. *Monographs of the Society for Research in Child Development*, **74**(1–111, Serial No. 293).

Nelson, K. (1973). Structure and strategy in learning to talk. *Monographs of the Society for Research in Child Development*, **38**(1–2, Serial No. 149).

Tomasello, M. (2000). Do young children have adult syntactic competence? *Cognition*, **74**, 209–253.

Waxman, S. R., & Lidz, J. L. (2006). Early word learning. In D. Kuhn & R. Siegler (Eds.), *Handbook of child psychology* (Vol. 2, 6th ed., pp. 299–335). Hoboken, NJ: Wiley.

EARLY VERB LEARNERS: CREATIVE OR NOT?

Jane B. Childers

This monograph describes a longitudinal study of eight children's first verb uses including an analysis of the variety of words used in conjunction with 34 targeted verbs, the variety of utterances produced, and the patterns of developmental change in the first 10 uses of these verbs. These data are important because most diary studies have included very few children at a time and have not focused on the beginnings of verb learning. Thus, these results advance our understanding of an early stage of verb learning that has received relatively little attention.

The main controversy discussed by the authors concerns the nature of the young verb learner as a creative user of language or as a more conservative one. Verb researchers tend to view the child on one side of this debate or the other and, of course, these differing world views influence the kinds of studies conducted and the ways in which data are interpreted. However, there are dangers to both overestimating or underestimating children's knowledge. If we assume more spontaneous creativity by the child than we should, we may begin down a path of experimentation that will ultimately be less fruitful than it would be, while if we ignore creativity that is present, we will miss revealing a capacity of the human mind that is profound. How to resolve this issue is unclear; however, the debate is likely to rage for some time.

Putting questions of how to view children's productions in this study aside for a moment, an important contribution of this study is that it sheds light on a stage of verb development that is relatively unexplored. Although a new focus of research is directed at understanding event understanding in infancy (e.g., Wagner & Lakusta, 2009), much of what is known about verb learning concerns children's comprehension and/or production after 24 months (e.g., Fisher, 2002; Theakston, Lieven, Pine, & Rowland, 2004). Thus, a better understanding of the initial stages of verb learning is needed. It is difficult to get children younger than 24 months to produce reliable verb utterances in the laboratory, and so sampling (or having their parent record) speech in everyday contexts provides data that to date have been scarce. On the other hand, a great advantage of experimental studies is that a researcher can control how many exposures a child has to a given verb, the specific sentences in which that particular verb has been heard, and the timing of those sentences. In one study in which these factors were controlled, 2.5-year-old children needed about a week of daily exposure to a verb to produce it (Childers & Tomasello, 2002). A limitation of laboratory studies is that they probably underestimate children's productive abilities because the child has to produce the new verb at the right time in an experimental setting. However, these kinds of studies (e.g., Abbot-Smith, Lieven, & Tomasello, 2004; Akhtar & Tomasello, 1997) are important for answering questions about children's ability to be productive, that is, their ability to extend a verb they have not heard in a particular sentence type to a new sentence type.

HOW CREATIVE ARE THESE CHILDREN'S PRODUCTIONS?

Flexibility in Verb Uses

An important question in verb learning concerns the scope of an individual verb's meaning early in development. A prevailing view is that children are initially context bound in their verb uses, producing verbs only in particular the situational contexts and failing to extending a new verb very widely (e.g., Huttenlocher, Smiley, & Charney, 1983); recent experimental evidence has partially supported this view (Forbes & Poulin-Dubois, 1997; Maguire, Hirsh-Pasek, Golinkoff, & Brandone, 2008). This type of conservativism would be very useful to children given the somewhat idiosyncratic nature of the meaning of an individual verb as well as the less organized structure of the verb category compared with the hierarchical structure of concrete nouns. Some of the analyses in this study included semantic flexibility, or the use of a verb with different nouns or in conjunction with different actions. These analyses are important because they show that young children are more flexible in the use of different affected object names than in their use of different agents and that both of these types of flexibility are more common than is flexibility across different actions (although uses across actions was difficult to code from these kinds of records). Thus, these results demonstrate that there are different levels of flexibility, even in the semantic domain, which is important. However, it is still unclear what the scope of meaning is like for these early verb representations because the analyses rest on children's productions of the new verbs, which are likely affected by a myriad of factors (e.g., objects available, motivation). In addition, even though new objects and agents were produced with the verbs (and these were the most common ways in which children were semantically flexible), it is possible that children were still using the verb in particular situational contexts (and, thus, were situationally bound), while mixing which particular entities in that context were named. That is, it is still somewhat unclear from these data how widely these new verbs were used across situational contexts, or how "portable" these verbs were. In my view, this is the kind of contextual boundedness others are reporting in early verb learning (e.g., Huttenlocher et al., 1983). In my laboratory, we are examining how children might achieve an appropriate level of "portability" (or extension) of a particular new verb by actively comparing the range of situations (Gentner, 1983, 1989) in which that verb is heard (Childers, in press; Childers & Paik, 2009).

Because all of the semantic flexibility exhibited in these children's utterances could have stemmed from uses by the adult, what that means in terms of children's *verb representations* is unclear. If children are using verbs to refer to different agents and to more than one action, but these are all initiated by the adult, could it be that a more superficial imitative process underlies this flexibility? That is, if the process underlying this semantic flexibility is imitative, could their verb representations remain fairly small, restricted, and context bound? This interpretation seems possible. Studies of verb use in everyday contexts are important because they can potentially reveal the breadth and depth of a young child's developing representation of a particular verb. This study provides some helpful data relevant for making inferences about what those representations are like, but a detailed coding of the situations in which a verb is produced (and perhaps whether a particular verb could have been produced but was not) is needed to reveal more fully the scope of children's early verb representations.

Obviously, children are likely to be *productive* in their verb uses at some point in development. Adults are productive verb users, creating new verbs (e.g., "texting") and extending existing patterns of use to those new words ("I'll text you later"). The debate centers on how early children are productive (i.e., spontaneously creative in ways that go beyond the input) because later productivity allows for the possibility that children could learn to be productive, while early productivity suggests mechanisms that support that creativity could be innate. These data do not bear directly on this question because, without the input, we are unable to discern how these children's flexible productions are tied to specific utterances they may have heard from an adult. That is, the question of productivity requires an evaluation of the strength of the link from parent speech to child speech. However, this limitation does not mean that these data are not important.

The question of whether children can go beyond the input in the early stages of verb learning will be difficult to test. It will be difficult to record all of the input for a particular verb and then compare it with the child's production of that verb to reveal new productions not heard. Other arguments of creativity in productions have included a discussion of errors made that would not fit the input and of errors that are possible but are never made. For example, Bowerman's (1982) description of verb errors in older children is important because, by these ages, her children were producing errors that did not fit anything an adult English speaker would say. In addition, laboratory studies in which exposure to the number and types of sentences in which a novel verb is heard, with methodologies that are sensitive to toddler abilities, make it possible to control the input and address the question of productivity. Given that we currently have very little of either type of data (diary or laboratory) for this stage of verb acquisition, a major contribution of the present study is that it demonstrates the kinds of flexibility children can produce in the early stages of verb learning, even though this flexibility may have direct links to specific utterances created by an adult.

Flexibility in Utterances

Even though flexibility is not the same as productivity, it is important that these researchers examined the utterances children produced and evaluated them for flexibility as well. These analyses show that these children were producing verbs in more than one type of utterance. However, most of the data reported here concern one- and two-word utterances, and thus it is unclear whether these utterances are scaffolded by an underlying structured grammar. Lois Bloom's (1993) and Martin Braine's (1971) work demonstrate the same tensions as reflected in this current work. For example, Braine pointed out that there are too few words in the utterances to be sure of whether the child has a grammatical category or does not. Thus, some of the differences between the present study and Tomasello (1992) reflect the tension between a rich (L. Bloom-like) interpretation of utterances as seen here and a more conservative analysis of utterances as used by Braine and Tomasello. (And, although we usually prize conservatism in science, as noted, being overly conservative has its own limitations.)

In addition, children were using utterances to command and to describe, but, at the same time, there are many more communicative functions that could be expressed. This could be viewed as pragmatic flexibility as Naigles and colleagues argue, or it could be viewed as a restricted set of communicative functions. These are just the type of utterances parents are likely to use frequently with young children: commands and descriptions of events. Thus, the tendency for children to use these forms could be evidence of a link between parent and child speech in this study.

Are Individual Differences Important?

Another major contribution made by this monograph is that it provides a sense of individual variation in verb learning in this sample. However, as Naigles and colleagues note, this range is not fully representative of the actual range of variation, or even of the range of parents who initially agreed to participate in this labor-intensive study. Instead, a surprising number of families initially agreed but found that their children were not producing verbs. In addition, several families began the study but had to drop out because their children were too verbal. Thus, the range represented here represents a midrange of children who were neither too verbal nor not verbal enough at the time of the study, and the interpretation of the results should be made with these participant characteristics in mind. Perhaps the variability in development in this study is even more surprising then, given the fact that children at each end of variation were not included. The careful analysis by these researchers provides important information about different trajectories children take in verb learning, which is important for researchers, parents, and speech therapists alike for understanding ways in which normal language development unfolds.

Are There Specific Verbs That Provide a Particular Benefit in Verb Learning?

Finally, the evidence presented in this monograph addresses questions about whether the acquisition of some verbs is more useful for breaking into the verb lexicon. An advantage nouns have over verbs is that the nouns that refer to concrete objects can be ordered hierarchically within a category. Thus, researchers can examine the acquisition of nouns at different levels of a hierarchy and have found an early tendency for children to learn nouns for entities at the basic level as opposed to the superordinate or subordinate levels (e.g., Rosch, 1978). Verbs in a language do not appear to have a clear basic level or a single hierarchical structure. There is a small set of verbs that is fairly general ("light verbs"). As Naigles and colleagues note, there are researchers who have proposed that this set is especially important in verb learning because these general verbs can help the child discover patterns of syntax that hold for groups of verbs. However, it has been unclear whether these verbs actually serve this function of "pathbreaking," and there is no evidence that they do so here. Even if this small set of very general (light) verbs does provide important data to the child, this is obviously not the same as the "basic level" in noun learning. Thus, instead of thinking of verb learning as proceeding along a particular dimension in a hierarchy, children appear to be learning both general and more specific verbs at the same time, as the study reported in this monograph demonstrates effectively. In addition, verbs seem to group into clusters of meaning, or clusters of verbs that share sets of syntactic frames, instead of being hierarchically structured

137

across the verb category, and thus it is unclear whether general extension strategies across different verbs would actually be useful. Children may be better served by being conservative in verb learning, given the major differences in the meaning of individual verbs and the differences in the range of syntactic frames that particular verbs allow.

CONCLUSION

The study reported here is important because it includes several children, focuses on early verb uses, and reveals information about those uses across semantic and syntactic contexts. Future studies are needed to clarify the scope of children's early verb representations and the relationship between parental input and children's productions. However, this study makes an important contribution to the field by revealing more about an early stage of verb learning that is poorly understood. Thus, this study provides an important link between studies of infants' event processing and studies of verb learning after 24 months, a link that is important for understanding the entirety of verb development.

References

Abbot-Smith, K., Lieven, E. V. M., & Tomasello, M. (2004). Training 2–6-year-olds to produce the transitive construction: The role of frequency, semantic similarity and shared syntactic distribution. *Developmental Science, 7*, 48–55.

Akhtar, N., & Tomasello, M. (1997). Young children's productivity with word order and verb morphology. *Developmental Psychology, 33*, 952–965.

Bloom, L. (1993). *Language development from two to three*. Cambridge, UK: Cambridge University Press.

Bowerman, M. (1982). Reorganizational processes in lexical and syntactic development. In L. Gleitman & E. Wanner (Eds.), *Language acquisition: The state of the art* (pp. 320–346). Cambridge, UK: Cambridge University Press.

Braine, M. D. S. (1971). On two types of models of the internalization of grammars. In D. I. Slobin (Ed.), *The ontogenesis of grammar* (pp. 153–186). New York: Academic Press.

Childers, J. B. (in press). Attention to multiple events helps two 1/2-year-olds extend new verbs. *First Language*.

Childers, J. B., & Paik, J. H. (2009). Korean- and English-speaking children use cross-situational information to learn novel predicate terms. *Journal of Child Language, 36*, 201–224.

Childers, J. B., & Tomasello, M. (2002). Two-year-olds learn novel nouns, verbs, and conventional actions from massed or spaced exposures. *Developmental Psychology, 38*, 967–978.

Fisher, C. (2002). Structural limits on verb mapping: The role of abstract structure in 2.5-year-olds' interpretations of novel verbs. *Developmental Science, 5*, 55–64.

Forbes, J. N., & Poulin-Dubois, D. (1997). Representational change in young children's understanding of familiar verb meaning. *Journal of Child Language*, **24**, 389–406.

Gentner, D. (1983). Structure-mapping: A theoretical framework for analogy. *Cognitive Science*, **7**, 155–170.

Gentner, D. (1989). The mechanisms of analogical learning. In S. Vosniadou & A. Ortony (Eds.), *Similarity and analogical reasoning* (pp. 199–241). New York: Cambridge University Press.

Huttenlocher, J., Smiley, P., & Charney, R. (1983). Emergence of action categories in the child: Evidence from verb meanings. *Psychological Review*, **90**, 72–93.

Maguire, M. J., Hirsh-Pasek, K., Golinkoff, R. M., & Brandone, A. C. (2008). Focusing on the relation: Fewer examples facilitate children's initial verb learning and extension. *Developmental Science*, **11**, 628–634.

Rosch, E. (1978). Principles of categorization. In E. Rosch & B. B. Lloyd (Eds.), *Cognition and categorization* (pp. 27–48). Hillsdale, NJ: Lawrence Erlbaum Associates.

Theakston, A. L., Lieven, E. V. M., Pine, J. M., & Rowland, C. F. (2004). Semantic generality, input frequency and the acquisition of syntax. *Journal of Child Language*, **31**, 61–99.

Tomasello, M. (1992). *First verbs: A case study of early grammatical development*. Cambridge, UK: Cambridge University Press.

Wagner, L., & Lakusta, L. (2009). Using language to navigate the infant mind. *Perspectives on Psychological Science*, **4**, 177–184.

CONTRIBUTORS

Letitia R. Naigles (Ph.D. 1988, University of Pennsylvania) is Professor of Psychology at the University of Connecticut. Her research investigates the processes of language acquisition in children with autism and compares language development across languages and cultures.

Erika Hoff (Ph.D. 1981, University of Michigan) is Professor of Psychology at Florida Atlantic University. Her research investigates the role of input in early language development and the relation of phonological memory to early lexical development in monolingual and bilingual children.

Donna Vear (M.A. 2002, University of Connecticut) is a children's clinician at NRI Community Services, Woonsocket, Rhode Island.

Michael Tomasello is the Director of the Max Planck Institute for Evolutionary Anthropology Department of Developmental and Comparative Psychology in Germany. His major research interests are in processes of social cognition, social learning, and communication from developmental, comparative, and cultural perspectives—especially aspects related to language and its acquisition. His current theoretical focus is on processes of shared intentionality. His empirical research involves mainly human children from 1 to 4 years of age and great apes.

Silke Brandt is a postdoctoral researcher at the Max Planck Institute for Evolutionary Anthropology. Dr. Brandt's research interests are in language acquisition in German and English, acquisition and processing of complex syntax, language and theory of mind, and general learning mechanisms.

Sandra R. Waxman is a professor in the Department of Psychology at Northwestern University. Her research is focused on the relation between language and conceptual development across development and across languages, and on the acquisition of biological knowledge and reasoning across cultures. She is a recent recipient of a Guggenheim Fellowship, the Ann L. Brown Award for Excellence in Developmental Research form the University of Illinois, and a James McKeen Cattell Award.

Jane B. Childers (Ph.D., 1998, University of Texas–Austin) is an Associate Professor of Psychology at Trinity University, San Antonio. The main focus of her research is to examine children's early verb learning, both in laboratory studies and in naturalistic contexts across cultures. Her current research examines how domain-general mechanisms, including comparison processes, may contribute to the acquisition of verbs.

STATEMENT OF EDITORIAL POLICY

The *Monographs* series aims to publish major reports of developmental research that generate authoritative new findings and uses these to foster a fresh perspective or integration of findings on some conceptually significant issue. Submissions from programmatic research projects are welcomed; these may consist of individually or group-authored reports of findings from a single large-scale investigation or from a sequence of experiments centering on a particular question. Multiauthored sets of independent studies that center on the same underlying question may also be appropriate; a critical requirement in such instances is that the various authors address common issues and that the contribution arising from the set as a whole be unique, substantial, and well-integrated. Manuscripts reporting interdisciplinary or multidisciplinary research on significant developmental questions and those including evidence from diverse cultural, racial, ethnic, national, or other contexts are of particular interest. Because the aim of the series is not only to advance knowledge on specialized topics but also to enhance cross-fertilization among disciplines or subfields, the links between the specific issues under study and larger questions relating to developmental processes should emerge clearly for both general readers and specialists on the topic. In short, irrespective of how it may be framed, work that contributes significant data or extends developmental thinking will be considered.

Potential authors are not required to be members of the Society for Research in Child Development or affiliated with the academic discipline of psychology to submit a manuscript for consideration by the *Monographs*. The significance of the work in extending developmental theory and in contributing new empirical information is the crucial consideration.

Submissions should contain a minimum of 80 manuscript pages (including tables and references). The upper boundary of 150–175 pages is more flexible, but authors should try to keep within this limit. If color artwork is submitted, and the authors believe color art is necessary to the presentation of their work, the submissions letter should indicate that one or more authors or their institutions are prepared to pay the substantial costs associated with color art reproduction. Please submit manuscripts electronically to the SRCD Monographs Online Submissions and Review Site (MONOSubmit) at www.srcd.org/monosubmit. Please contact the Monographs office with any questions at monographs@srcd.org.

The corresponding author for any manuscript must, in the submission letter, warrant that all coauthors are in agreement with the content of the manuscript. The corresponding author also is responsible for informing all coauthors, in a timely manner, of manuscript submission, editorial decisions, reviews received, and any revisions recommended. Before publication, the corresponding author must warrant in the submissions letter that the study was conducted according to the ethical guidelines of the Society for Research in Child Development.

Potential authors who may be unsure whether the manuscript they are planning would make an appropriate submission are invited to draft an outline of what they propose and send it to the editor for assessment. This mechanism, as well as a more detailed description of all editorial policies, evaluation processes, and format requirements, is given in the "Guidelines for the Preparation of Publication Submissions," which can be found at the SRCD website by clicking on *Monographs*, or by contacting the editor, W. Andrew Collins, Institute of Child Development, University of Minnesota, 51 E. River Road, Minneapolis, MN 55455-0345; e-mail: wcollins@umn.edu.

Note to NIH Grantees

Pursuant to NIH mandate, Society through Wiley-Blackwell will post the accepted version of Contributions authored by NIH grantholders to PubMed Central upon acceptance. This accepted version will be made publicly available 12 months after publication. For further information, see www.wiley.com/go/nihmandate.

CURRENT